CoffeeScript Programming with jQuery, Rails, and Node.js

Learn CoffeeScript programming with the three most popular web technologies around

Michael Erasmus

BIRMINGHAM - MUMBAI

CoffeeScript Programming with jQuery, Rails, and Node.js

First published: December 2012

Production Reference: 1061212

Published by Packt Publishing Ltd.
Livery Place
35 Livery Street
Birmingham B3 2PB, UK.

ISBN 978-1-84951-958-8

www.packtpub.com

Cover Image by Abhishek Pandey (abhishek.pandey1210@gmail.com)

Credits

Author
Michael Erasmus

Reviewers
Stephen Ball
Shreyank Gupta

Acquisition Editor
Mary Jasmine

Commissioning Editor
Meeta Rajani

Technical Editor
Dominic Pereira

Copy Editor
Alfida Paiva

Project Coordinator
Shraddha Bagadia

Proofreader
Maria Gould

Indexer
Hemangini Bari

Production Coordinator
Prachali Bhiwandkar

Cover Work
Prachali Bhiwandkar

About the Author

Michael Erasmus has been developing software for over 10 years. He has been a C# programmer for quite a few of them, but has luckily been enlightened enough to become an open source zealot during the last few years. The most loved tools in his utility belt are Ruby and Rails, Linux, MongoDB, Vim, jQuery, and CoffeeScript.

He's interested in all manner of science and technology, but tends to dwell on things such as elegant and eccentric programming languages, machine learning and statistics, web development, Internet startups, and civic hacking.

He is currently working at `22seven.com`, building a service that will help change people's behavior and do more with the money they have.

When he's not sitting in front of the computer, he likes pulling faces to amuse his baby son, apologizing to his wonderful wife for sitting in front of a computer all day, or arguing endlessly with friends, family, colleagues, and random strangers. He lives near the beach in Muizenberg, Cape Town and loves it.

I would like to thank my wonderful wife for supporting me in all my crazy endeavors and always being there when things get tough. Thanks to my employers and colleagues for their support and feedback. I would also like to express my gratitude to the open source community in general, and for everyone out there selflessly sharing your work.

About the Reviewers

Stephen Ball works for PhishMe Inc. as a full stack Rails developer. He started programming in BASIC in the 80s and has been tinkering on the Internet since the early 90s. He's programming for the Web in Perl, PHP, Python, Django, Node.js, and Rails. He currently writes a Ruby and Rails blog at `http://rakeroutes.com` and a CoffeeScript blog at `http://coffeescriptcafe.com`. He lives with his wife, Sarah, and two children, Edward and Marie, in Durham, NC, USA.

Shreyank Gupta is a passout of NIT Durgapur. He works as a programmer and web developer at Red Hat since 2009. In his free time he works on improving his photography.

www.PacktPub.com

Support files, eBooks, discount offers and more

You might want to visit www.PacktPub.com for support files and downloads related to your book.

Did you know that Packt offers eBook versions of every book published, with PDF and ePub files available? You can upgrade to the eBook version at www.PacktPub.com and as a print book customer, you are entitled to a discount on the eBook copy. Get in touch with us at service@packtpub.com for more details.

At www.PacktPub.com, you can also read a collection of free technical articles, sign up for a range of free newsletters and receive exclusive discounts and offers on Packt books and eBooks.

http://PacktLib.PacktPub.com

Do you need instant solutions to your IT questions? PacktLib is Packt's online digital book library. Here, you can access, read and search across Packt's entire library of books.

Why Subscribe?

- Fully searchable across every book published by Packt
- Copy and paste, print and bookmark content
- On demand and accessible via web browser

Free Access for Packt account holders

If you have an account with Packt at www.PacktPub.com, you can use this to access PacktLib today and view nine entirely free books. Simply use your login credentials for immediate access.

Table of Contents

Preface **1**

Chapter 1: Why CoffeeScript? **7**

CoffeeScript syntax **8**
Semicolons and braces 9
Whitespace 9
Parenthesis 10
CoffeeScript has great function syntax **11**
Return isn't required 12
Function arguments 12
Where did the var keyword go? 13
CoffeeScript handles scope better **14**
Top level var keywords 15
CoffeeScript has better object syntax **16**
Inheritance 17
Overwhelmed? 18
Extending prototypes 18
A few other things CoffeeScript fixes **18**
Reserved words and object syntax 19
String concatenation 21
Equality 21
The existential operator 22
List comprehensions **24**
The while loop 24
Conditional clauses and logical aliases **28**
Array slicing and splicing **29**
Destructuring or pattern matching **30**
=> and @ **33**
Switch statements **35**

Chained comparisons **36**
Block strings, block comments, and strings **36**
Summary **36**
Chapter 2: Running CoffeeScript **39**
The CoffeeScript stack **39**
Node.js and npm **40**
Node.js, npm, and CoffeeScript on Windows **41**
Installing CoffeeScript on a Mac **44**
Using the Apple installer 44
Using Homebrew 46
Installing CoffeeScript with npm 47
Installing CoffeeScript on Linux **48**
Ubuntu and MintOS 48
Debian 48
Other distributions 48
Installing CoffeeScript with npm 49
Building Node.js from source **49**
Building on Linux or Unix 49
Building on Windows 50
Using CoffeeScript **51**
The coffee command **51**
The REPL 52
Running .coffee files 52
Compiling to JavaScript 53
Watching 53
Putting it all together 53
Summary **54**
Chapter 3: CoffeeScript and jQuery **55**
Finding and changing elements **56**
The $ function 56
Utility functions **57**
Ajax methods **58**
Using jQuery **58**
Using CoffeeScript and jQuery in the browser **58**
Compiling CoffeeScript 58
jQuery and CoffeeScript 59
Testing it all 60
Running a local web server 61
Our application **61**
TodoMVC 62

Our initial HTML 62
Initializing our app 63
Adding a to-do item 64
Using localStorage 64
Displaying the to-do items 66
Showing the to-do items 69
Removing and completing items 70
Now, it's your turn! 71
Summary 71
Chapter 4: CoffeeScript and Rails 73
What makes Rails special? 73
Convention over configuration 73
Don't repeat yourself (DRY) 74
Rails and JavaScript 74
Rails and CoffeeScript 75
Installing Rails 76
Installing Rails using RailsInstaller 76
Installing Rails using RVM 76
Got Rails installed? 77
Developing our Rails application 77
MVC 78
Running our application 78
Our todo_items resource 79
routes.rb 80
The controller 80
The view 81
The CSS 82
Our model 83
Migrations 84
The Rails console 85
Displaying the items in our view using ERB 87
Creating a partial 88
Adding new items 89
Let's try and add a to-do item 90
Adding a CoffeeScript view 91
CoffeeScript in the asset pipeline 91
Completing the to-do items 92
Removing tasks 93
Now, it's your turn 93
Summary 94

Chapter 5: CoffeeScript and Node.js **95**
Node is event-driven **95**
Node is fast and scalable **96**
Node is not Rails **96**
Node and CoffeeScript **96**
"Hello World" in Node **96**
Express **97**
WebSocket **97**
Jade **98**
Our application **98**
Let's get started **98**
package.json 99
Installing our modules 99
Creating our app 100
Running our application 100
Creating a view **101**
node-supervisor **102**
The to-do list view **103**
Middleware 104
Our stylesheet 104
The client side **105**
Adding collaboration **108**
Creating the collaboration UI **108**
WebSocket on the client **109**
WebSocket on the server **110**
Joining a list **111**
The UI 112
Leaving a list 114
Testing it all 115
Adding to-do items to a shared list **116**
Removing to-do items from a shared list **118**
Now, it's your turn 120
Summary **120**
Index **121**

Preface

JavaScript is a quirky little language that was written by Brendan Eich when he was working at Netscape around 1995. It was the first browser-based scripting language and ran only in Netscape Navigator at the time, but it eventually found its way into most other web browsers. Back then, web pages consisted almost entirely of static markup. JavaScript (initially named LiveScript) emerged around the need to make pages dynamic and to bring the power of a full scripting language to browser developers.

A lot of the design decisions of the language were driven by the need of simplicity and ease of use, although at the time, some were made for pure marketing reasons at Netscape. The name "JavaScript" was chosen to associate it with Java from Sun Microsystems, despite the fact that Sun really had nothing to do with it and that it's conceptually quite different from its namesake.

Except in one way, that is, most of its syntax was borrowed from Java, and also C and C++, so as to be familiar to the programmers coming from these languages. But despite looking similar, it is in fact a very different beast under the hood and shares characteristics with the more exotic languages such as Self, Scheme, and Smalltalk. Among these are dynamic typing, prototypical inheritance, first class functions, and closures.

So we ended up with a language that looked a lot like some of the mainstream languages at the time and could be coaxed into acting a lot like them, but with quite different central ideas. This has caused it to be very misunderstood for many years. A lot of programmers never saw it as being a "serious" programming language and thus didn't apply a lot of the best development practices built up over decades when it came to writing browser code.

Those who did delve further into the language were sure to find a lot of strangeness. Eich himself admitted that the language was prototyped within about 10 days, and even though what he came up with was impressive, JavaScript isn't without (many) warts. These too didn't really help to raise its profile.

Despite all these issues, JavaScript still became one of the most widely used programming languages in the world, if not merely because of the explosion of the Internet and the spread of web browsers. Support across a multitude of browsers would seem to be a great thing, but it also caused havoc because of differences in implementations, both in the language and the DOM.

Around 2005, the term AJAX was coined to describe a style of JavaScript programming that was made possible by the introduction of the `XMLHTTPRequest` object in browsers. This meant that developers could write client-side code that could communicate with the server using HTTP directly, and update page elements without reloading the page. This was really a turning point in the history of the language. All of a sudden, it was being used in "serious" web applications, and people began to see the language in a different light.

In 2006, John Resig released jQuery to the world. It was designed to simplify client-side scripting, DOM manipulation, and AJAX, as well as to abstract away many of the inconsistencies across browsers. It became an essential tool for many JavaScript programmers. To date, it is used on 55 percent of the top 10, 000 websites in the world.

In 2009, Ryan Dahl created Node.js, an event-driven network application framework written on top of the Google V8 JavaScript engine. It quickly became very popular, especially for writing web server applications. A big factor in its success has been the fact that you could now write JavaScript on the server, as well as in the browser. An elaborate and distinguished community has sprung up around the framework, and at present the future of Node.js is looking very bright.

Early in 2010, Jeremy Ashkenas created CoffeeScript, a language that compiles to JavaScript. Its goal is to create cleaner, more concise, and more idiomatic JavaScript and to make it easier to use the better features and patterns of the language. It does away with a lot of the syntactic cruft of JavaScript, reducing the line noise and generally creating much shorter and clearer code.

Influenced by languages such as Ruby, Python, and Haskell, it borrows some of the powerful and interesting features of these languages. Although it can look quite different, the CoffeeScript code generally maps to its generated JavaScript pretty closely. It has grown to be an overnight success, quickly being adopted by the Node.js community as well as being included in Ruby on Rails 3.1.

Brendan Eich has also expressed his admiration for CoffeeScript, and has used it as an example of some of the things he would like to see in the future versions of JavaScript.

This book serves as an introduction to the language as well as a motivation for why you should write CoffeeScript instead of JavaScript wherever you can. It also then explores using CoffeeScript in the browser using jQuery and Ruby on Rails, as well as on the server using Node.js.

What this book covers

Chapter 1, Why CoffeeScript?, introduces CoffeeScript and delves deeper into the differences between it and JavaScript, specifically focusing on the parts of JavaScript that CoffeeScript aims to improve.

Chapter 2, Running CoffeeScript, goes into a short introduction of the CoffeeScript stack and how it's typically packaged. You will learn how to install CoffeeScript on Windows, Mac, and Linux using Node.js and npm. You will get to know the CoffeeScript compiler (`coffee`) as well as get familiar with some helpful tools and resources for day-to-day development in CoffeeScript.

Chapter 3, CoffeeScript and jQuery, introduces client-side development using jQuery and CoffeeScript. We also start implementing a sample application for this book using these technologies.

Chapter 4, CoffeeScript and Rails, starts with a brief overview of Ruby on Rails, and its history with JavaScript frameworks. We are introduced to the Asset Pipeline in Rails 3.1 and how it integrates with CoffeeScript and jQuery. We then move to adding a backend to our sample application using Rails.

Chapter 5, CoffeeScript and Node.js, starts with a brief overview of Node.js, its history, and philosophy. It then demonstrates how easy it is to write server-side code in CoffeeScript using Node.js. We then implement the final piece of the sample application using WebSockets and Node.js.

What you need for this book

To use this book, you need a computer running Windows, Mac OS X, or Linux and a basic text editor. Throughout the book, we'll be downloading some software that we need from the Internet, all of which will be free and open source.

Who this book is for

This book is for existing JavaScript programmers who would like to learn more about CoffeeScript, or someone who has some programming experience and would like to learn more about web development using CoffeeScript. It also serves as a great introduction to jQuery, Ruby on Rails, and Node.js. Even if you have experience with one or more of these frameworks, this book will show you how you can use CoffeeScript to make your experiences with them even better.

Conventions

In this book, you will find a number of styles of text that distinguish between different kinds of information. Here are some examples of these styles, and an explanation of their meaning.

Code words in text are shown as follows: "You'll see that the clause of the `if` statement does not need be enclosed within parentheses".

A block of code is set as follows:

```
gpaScoreAverage = (scores...) ->
   total = scores.reduce (a, b) -> a + b
   total / scores.length
```

When we wish to draw your attention to a particular part of a code block, the relevant lines or items are set in bold:

```
create: (e) ->
    $input = $(event.target)
    val = ($.trim $input.val())
```

Any command-line input or output is written as follows:

```
coffee -co public/js -w src/
```

New terms and **important words** are shown in bold. Words that you see on the screen, in menus or dialog boxes for example, appear in the text like this: "a footer will have the **Clear completed** button".

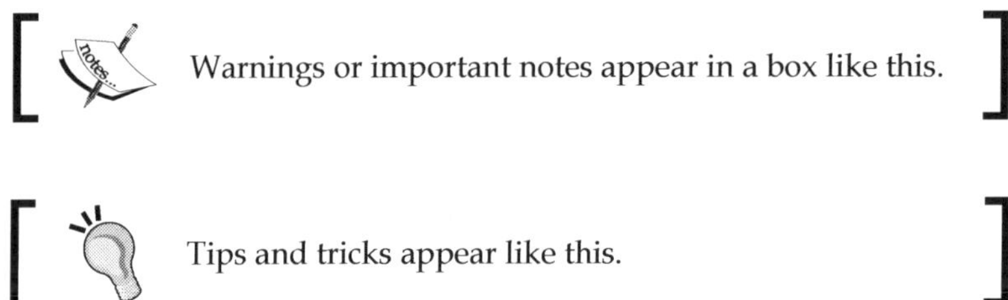

Reader feedback

Feedback from our readers is always welcome. Let us know what you think about this book—what you liked or may have disliked. Reader feedback is important for us to develop titles that you really get the most out of.

To send us general feedback, simply send an e-mail to `feedback@packtpub.com`, and mention the book title via the subject of your message.

If there is a topic that you have expertise in and you are interested in either writing or contributing to a book, see our author guide on `www.packtpub.com/authors`.

Customer support

Now that you are the proud owner of a Packt book, we have a number of things to help you to get the most from your purchase.

Downloading the example code

You can download the example code files for all Packt books you have purchased from your account at `http://www.PacktPub.com`. If you purchased this book elsewhere, you can visit `http://www.PacktPub.com/support` and register to have the files e-mailed directly to you.

Errata

Although we have taken every care to ensure the accuracy of our content, mistakes do happen. If you find a mistake in one of our books—maybe a mistake in the text or the code—we would be grateful if you would report this to us. By doing so, you can save other readers from frustration and help us improve subsequent versions of this book. If you find any errata, please report them by visiting `http://www.packtpub.com/support`, selecting your book, clicking on the **errata submission form** link, and entering the details of your errata. Once your errata are verified, your submission will be accepted and the errata will be uploaded on our website, or added to any list of existing errata, under the Errata section of that title. Any existing errata can be viewed by selecting your title from `http://www.packtpub.com/support`.

Piracy

Piracy of copyright material on the Internet is an ongoing problem across all media. At Packt, we take the protection of our copyright and licenses very seriously. If you come across any illegal copies of our works, in any form, on the Internet, please provide us with the location address or website name immediately so that we can pursue a remedy.

Please contact us at `copyright@packtpub.com` with a link to the suspected pirated material.

We appreciate your help in protecting our authors, and our ability to bring you valuable content.

Questions

You can contact us at `questions@packtpub.com` if you are having a problem with any aspect of the book, and we will do our best to address it.

1
Why CoffeeScript?

CoffeeScript compiles to JavaScript and follows its idioms closely. It's quite possible to rewrite any CoffeeScript code in Javascript and it won't look drastically different. So why would you want to use CoffeeScript?

As an experienced JavaScript programmer, you might think that learning a completely new language is simply not worth the time and effort.

But ultimately, code is for programmers. The compiler doesn't care how the code looks or how clear its meaning is; either it will run or it won't. We aim to write expressive code as programmers so that we can read, reference, understand, modify, and rewrite it.

If the code is too complex or filled with needless ceremony, it will be harder to understand and maintain. CoffeeScript gives us an advantage to clarify our ideas and write more readable code.

It's a misconception to think that CoffeeScript is very different from JavaScript. There might be some drastic syntax differences here and there, but in essence, CoffeeScript was designed to polish the rough edges of JavaScript to reveal the beautiful language hidden beneath. It steers programmers towards JavaScript's so-called "good parts" and holds strong opinions of what constitutes good JavaScript.

One of the mantras of the CoffeeScript community is: "It's just JavaScript", and I have also found that the best way to truly comprehend the language is to look at how it generates its output, which is actually quite readable and understandable code.

Throughout this chapter, we'll highlight some of the differences between the two languages, often focusing on the things in JavaScript that CoffeeScript tries to improve.

In this way, I would not only like to give you an overview of the major features of the language, but also prepare you to be able to debug your CoffeeScript from its generated code once you start using it more often, as well as being able to convert existing JavaScript.

Let's start with some of the things CoffeeScript fixes in JavaScript.

CoffeeScript syntax

One of the great things about CoffeeScript is that you tend to write much shorter and more succinct programs than you normally would in JavaScript. Some of this is because of the powerful features added to the language, but it also makes a few tweaks to the general syntax of JavaScript to transform it to something quite elegant. It does away with all the semicolons, braces, and other cruft that usually contributes to a lot of the "line noise" in JavaScript.

To illustrate this, let's look at an example. On the left-hand side of the following table is CoffeeScript; on the right-hand side is the generated JavaScript:

<table>
<tr><th>CoffeeScript</th><th>JavaScript</th></tr>
<tr><td>

```
fibonacci = (n) ->
 return 0 if n == 0
 return 1 if n == 1
 (fibonacci n-1) +
(fibonacci n-2)

alert fibonacci 10
```

</td><td>

```
var fibonacci;

fibonacci = function(n) {
  if (n === 0) {
    return 0;
  }
  if (n === 1) {
    return 1;
  }
  return (fibonacci(n - 1))
+ (fibonacci(n - 2));
};

alert(fibonacci(10));
```

</td></tr>
</table>

To run the code examples in this chapter, you can use the great **Try CoffeeScript** online tool, at `http://coffeescript.org`. It allows you to type in CoffeeScript code, which will then display the equivalent JavaScript in a side pane. You can also run the code right from the browser (by clicking the **Run** button in the upper-left corner). If you prefer to get CoffeeScript running on your computer to run the samples first, skip to the next chapter and then come back once you have CoffeeScript installed. This tool is shown in the following screenshot:

At first, the two languages might appear to be quite drastically different, but hopefully as we go through the differences, you'll see that it's all still JavaScript with some small tweaks and a lot of nice syntactical sugar.

Semicolons and braces

As you might have noticed, CoffeeScript does away with all the trailing semicolons at the end of a line. You can still use a semicolon if you want to put two expressions on a single line. It also does away with enclosing braces (also known as curly brackets) for code blocks such as `if` statements, `switch`, and the `try..catch` block.

Whitespace

You might be wondering how the parser figures out where your code blocks start and end. The CoffeeScript compiler does this by using syntactical whitespace. This means that indentation is used for delimited code blocks instead of braces.

This is perhaps one of the most controversial features of the language. If you think about it, in almost all languages, programmers tend to already use indentation of code blocks to improve readability, so why not make it part of the syntax? This is not a new concept, and was mostly borrowed from Python. If you have any experience with significant whitespace language, you will not have any trouble with CoffeeScript indentation.

If you don't, it might take some getting used to, but it makes for code that is wonderfully readable and easy to scan, while shaving off quite a few keystrokes. I'm willing to bet that if you do take the time to get over some initial reservations you might have, you might just grow to love block indentation.

Blocks can be indented with tabs or spaces, but be careful about being consistent using one or the other, or CoffeeScript will not be able to parse your code correctly.

Parenthesis

You'll see that the clause of the `if` statement does not need be enclosed within parentheses. The same goes for the `alert` function; you'll see that the single string parameter follows the function call without parentheses as well. In CoffeeScript, parentheses are optional in function calls with parameters, clauses for `if..else` statements, as well as `while` loops.

Although functions with arguments do not need parentheses, it is still a good idea to use them in cases where ambiguity might exist. The CoffeeScript community has come up with a nice idiom: wrapping the whole function call in parenthesis. The use of the `alert` function in CoffeeScript is shown in the following table:

CoffeeScript	JavaScript
`alert square 2 * 2.5 + 1`	`alert(square(2 * 2.5 + 1));`
`alert (square 2 * 2.5) + 1`	`alert((square(2 * 2.5)) + 1);`

Functions are first class objects in JavaScript. This means that when you refer to a function without parentheses, it will return the function itself, as a value. Thus, in CoffeeScript you still need to add parentheses when calling a function with no arguments.

By making these few tweaks to the syntax of JavaScript, CoffeeScript arguably already improves the readability and succinctness of your code by a big factor, and also saves you quite a lot of keystrokes.

But it has a few other tricks up its sleeve. Most programmers who have written a fair amount of JavaScript would probably agree that one of the phrases that gets typed the most frequently would have to be the function definition `function(){}`. Functions are really at the heart of JavaScript, yet not without its many warts.

CoffeeScript has great function syntax

The fact that you can treat functions as first class objects as well as being able to create anonymous functions is one of JavaScript's most powerful features. However, the syntax can be very awkward and make the code hard to read (especially if you start nesting functions). But CoffeeScript has a fix for this. Have a look at the following snippets:

CoffeeScript	JavaScript

`-> alert 'hi there!'`
`square = (n) -> n * n`
	`var square;`
	`(function() {`
	`  return alert('hi there!');`
	`});`
	`square = function(n) {`
	`  return n * n;`
	`};`

Here, we are creating two anonymous functions, the first just displays a dialog and the second will return the square of its argument. You've probably noticed the funny `->` symbol and might have figured out what it does. Yep, that is how you define a function in CoffeeScript. I have come across a couple of different names for the symbol but the most accepted term seems to be a thin arrow or just an arrow. This is as opposed to the fat arrow, which we'll discuss later.

Notice that the first function definition has no arguments and thus we can drop the parenthesis. The second function does have a single argument, which is enclosed in parenthesis, which goes in front of the `->` symbol. With what we now know, we can formulate a few simple substitution rules to convert JavaScript function declarations to CoffeeScript. They are as follows:

- Replace the `function` keyword with `->`
- If the function has no arguments, drop the parenthesis
- If it has arguments, move the whole argument list with parenthesis in front of the `->` symbol
- Make sure that the function body is properly indented and then drop the enclosing braces

Return isn't required

You might have noted that in both the functions, we left out the `return` keyword. By default, CoffeeScript will return the last expression in your function. It will try to do this in all the paths of execution. CoffeeScript will try turning any statement (fragment of code that returns nothing) into an expression that returns a value. CoffeeScript programmers will often refer to this feature of the language by saying that everything is an expression.

This means you don't need to type `return` anymore, but keep in mind that this can, in many cases, alter your code subtly, because of the fact that you will always return something. If you need to return a value from a function before the last statement, you can still use `return`.

Function arguments

Function arguments can also take an optional default value. In the following code snippet you'll see that the optional value specified is assigned in the body of the generated Javascript:

CoffeeScript	JavaScript

`square = (n=1) ->`
`  alert(n * n)`
	`var square;`
	
	`square = function(n) {`
	`  if (n == null) {`
	`    n = 1;`
	`  }`
	`  return alert(n * n);`
	`};`

In JavaScript, each function has an array-like structure called `arguments` with an indexed property for each argument that was passed to the function. You can use `arguments` to pass in a variable number of parameters to a function. Each parameter will be an element in arguments and thus you don't have to refer to parameters by name.

Although the `arguments` object acts somewhat like an array, it is in not in fact a "real" array and lacks most of the standard array methods. Often, you'll find that `arguments` doesn't provide the functionality needed to inspect and manipulate its elements like they are used with an array.

This has forced many programmers to use a hack by making `Array.prototype.slice` copy the `argument` object elements, or to use the `jQuery.makeArray` method to create a standard array, which can then be used like normal.

CoffeeScript borrows this pattern of creating an array from arguments that are represented by **splats**, denoted with three dots (`...`). These are shown in the following code snippet:

CoffeeScript:

```
gpaScoreAverage = (scores...) ->
   total = scores.reduce (a, b) -> a + b
   total / scores.length

alert gpaScoreAverage(65,78,81)
scores = [78, 75, 79]
alert gpaScoreAverage(scores...)
```

JavaScript:

```
var gpaScoreAverage, scores,
  __slice = [].slice;

gpaScoreAverage = function() {
  var scores, total;
  scores = 1 <= arguments.length ? __slice.call(arguments, 0) : [];
  total = scores.reduce(function(a, b) {
    return a + b;
  });
  return total / scores.length;
};

alert(gpaScoreAverage(65, 78, 81));
scores = [78, 75, 79];
alert(gpaScoreAverage.apply(null, scores));
```

Notice that in the function definition, the parameter is followed by `...`. This tells CoffeeScript to allow for variable arguments. The function can then be invoked using either a list of parameters or an array followed by `...`.

Where did the var keyword go?

In JavaScript, you create local variables by prefixing their declarations with a `var` keyword. If you omit it, the variable will be created in the global scope.

You'll see throughout these examples that that we didn't need to use the `var` keyword, and that CoffeeScript created the actual variable declarations at the top of the function in the generated JavaScript.

If you're an experienced JavaScripter, you might be wondering how you would then go about creating global variables. The simple answer is you can't.

Many people (probably including the authors of CoffeeScript) would argue that this is a good thing, because in most cases global variables should be avoided. Don't fret though, as there are ways to create top-level objects that we'll get to in a moment. But this does lead us neatly onto another benefit of CoffeeScript.

CoffeeScript handles scope better

Take a look at the following snippet of JavaScript. Notice that a variable called `salutation` gets defined in two places, inside the function, as well as after the function gets called the first time:

JavaScript

```
var greet = function(){
    if(typeof salutation === 'undefined')
        salutation = 'Hi!';
    console.log(salutation);
}
greet();
salutation = "Bye!";
greet();
```

In JavaScript, when you omit the `var` keyword while declaring a variable, it immediately becomes a global variable. Global variables are available in all scopes, and thus can be overwritten from anywhere, which often ends up as being a mess.

In the previous example, the `greet` function first checks if the `salutation` variable is defined (by checking if `typeof` equals `undefined`, a common workaround to see if a variable is defined in JavaScript). If it has not been defined previously, it creates it without a `var` keyword. This will immediately promote the variable to the global scope. We can see the consequences of this in the rest of the snippet.

The first time the `greet` function is called, the string **Hi!** will be logged. After the salutation has been changed and the function is called again, the console will instead log **Bye!**. Because the variable was leaked to be a global variable, its value was overwritten outside of the function scope.

This odd "feature" of the language has been the cause of many a headache for some weary programmer who forgot to include a `var` keyword somewhere. Even if you mean to declare a global variable, it is generally considered to be a bad design choice, which is why CoffeeScript disallows it.

CoffeeScript will always add the `var` keyword to any variable declaration to make sure that it doesn't inadvertently end up as a global declaration. In fact, you should never type `var` yourself, and the compiler will complain if you do.

Top level var keywords

When you declare a `var` normally at the top level of your script in JavaScript, it will still be available globally. This can also cause havoc when you include a bunch of different JavaScript files, since you might overwrite variables declared in earlier scripts.

In JavaScript and subsequently CoffeeScript, functions act as closures, meaning that they create their own variable scope as well as having their enclosing scope variables available to them.

Throughout the years, a common pattern started to emerge where library authors wrap their entire script in an anonymous closure function that they assign to a single variable.

The CoffeeScript compiler does something similar, and will wrap scripts in an anonymous function to avoid leaking its scope. In the following sample, the JavaScript is the output of running the CoffeeScript compiler:

CoffeeScript

```
greet = -> salutation = 'Hi!'
```

JavaScript

```
(var greet;
greet = function() {
  var salutation;
  return salutation = 'Hi!';
}).call(this);
```

Here you can see how CoffeeScript has wrapped the function definition in its own scope.

There are, however, certain cases where you would want a variable to be available throughout your application. Usually attaching a property to an existing global object can do this. When you're in the browser, you can just create a property on the global `window` object.

In browser-side JavaScript, the `window` object represents an open window. It's globally available to all other objects and thus can be used as a global namespace or container for other objects.

While we are on the subject of objects, let's talk about another part of JavaScript that CoffeeScript makes much better: defining and using objects.

CoffeeScript has better object syntax

The JavaScript language has a wonderful and unique object model, but the syntax and semantics for creating objects and inheriting from them has always been a bit cumbersome and widely misunderstood.

CoffeeScript cleans this up in a simple and elegant syntax that does not stray too far from idiomatic JavaScript. The following code demonstrates how CoffeeScript compiles its class syntax into JavaScript:

CoffeeScript:

```
class Vehicle
  constructor: ->
  drive: (km) ->
    alert "Drove #{km} kilometres"

bus = new Vehicle()
bus.drive 5
```

JavaScript:

```
var Vehicle, bus;
Vehicle = (function() {
  function Vehicle() {}
  Vehicle.prototype.drive = function(km) {
    return alert("Drove " + km + " kilometres");
  };
  return Vehicle;
})();
bus = new Vehicle();
bus.drive(5);
```

In CoffeeScript, you use the `class` keyword to define object structures. Under the hood, this creates a function object with function methods added to its prototype. The `constructor: operator` will create a constructor function that will be called when your object gets initialized with the `new` keyword.

All the other function methods are declared using the `methodName: () ->` syntax. These are created on the prototype of the object.

Did you notice the `#{km}` in our alert string? This is the string interpolation syntax, which was borrowed from Ruby. We'll talk about this later in the chapter.

Inheritance

What about object inheritance? Although it's possible, normally this is such a pain in JavaScript that most programmers don't even bother, or use a third-party library with non-standard semantics.

In this example you can see how CoffeeScript makes object inheritance elegant:

CoffeeScript:

```
class Car extends Vehicle
  constructor: ->
    @odometer = 0
  drive: (km) ->
    @odometer += km
    super km
car = new Car
car.drive 5
car.drive 8

alert "Odometer is at #{car.odometer}"
```

JavaScript:

```
Car = (function(_super) {
  __extends(Car, _super);
  function Car() {
    this.odometer = 0;
  }
  Car.prototype.drive = function(km) {
    this.odometer += km;
    return Car.__super__.drive.call(this, km);
  };
  return Car;
})(Vehicle);
```

```
car = new Car;
car.drive(5);
car.drive(8);
alert("Odometer is at " + car.odometer);
```

This example does not contain all the JavaScript code that will be generated by the compiler, but has enough to highlight the interesting parts. The `extends` operator is used to set up the inheritance chain between two objects and their constructors. Notice how much simpler the call to the parent class becomes with `super`.

As you can see, `@odometer` was translated to `this.odometer`. The `@` symbol is just a shortcut for `this`. We'll talk about it further on in this chapter.

Overwhelmed?

The `class` syntax is, in my opinion, where you'll find the greatest difference between CoffeeScript and its compiled JavaScript. However, most of the time it just works and once you understand it you'll rarely have to worry about the details.

Extending prototypes

If you're an experienced JavaScript programmer who still likes to do all of this yourself, you don't need to use `class`. CoffeeScript still provides the helpful shortcut to get at prototypes through the `::` symbol, which will be replaced by `.prototype` in the generated JavaScript, as shown in the following code snippet:

CoffeeScript	JavaScript
`Vehicle::stop=-> alert'Stopped'`	`Vehicle.prototype.stop(function() { return alert('Stopped'); });`

A few other things CoffeeScript fixes

JavaScript has lots of other small annoyances that CoffeeScript makes nicer. Let's have a look at some of these.

Reserved words and object syntax

Often in JavaScript, you will need to make use of a reserved word, or a keyword that is used by JavaScript. This often happens with keys for literal objects as data in JavaScript, like `class` or `for`, which you then need to enclose in quotes. CoffeeScript will automatically quote reserved words for you, and generally you don't even need to worry about it.

CoffeeScript	JavaScript

<pre>tag =
  type: 'label'
  name: 'nameLabel'
  for: 'name'
  class: 'label'</pre>
	<pre>var tag;
	
	tag = {
	  type: 'label',
	  name: 'nameLabel',
	  "for": 'name',
	  "class": 'label'
	};</pre>

Notice that we don't need the braces to create object literals and can use indentation here as well. While using this style, as long as there is only one property per line, we can drop the trailing commas too.

We can also write array literals in this way:

CoffeeScript	JavaScript

<pre>dwarfs = [
  "Sneezy"
  "Sleepy"
  "Dopey"
  "Doc"
  "Happy"
  "Bashful"
  "Grumpy"
]</pre>
	<pre>var dwarfs;
	
	dwarfs = ["Sneezy", "Sleepy",
	"Dopey", "Doc", "Happy",
	"Bashful", "Grumpy"];</pre>

These features combined make writing JSON a breeze. Compare the following samples to see the difference:

CoffeeScript:

```
"firstName": "John"
"lastName": "Smith"
"age": 25
"address":
  "streetAddress": "21 2nd Street"
  "city": "New York"
  "state": "NY"
  "postalCode": "10021"
"phoneNumber": [
  {"type": "home", "number": "212 555-1234"}
  {"type": "fax", "number": "646 555-4567"}
]
```

JavaScript:

```
({
  "firstName": "John",
  "lastName": "Smith",
  "age": 25,
  "address": {
    "streetAddress": "21 2nd Street",
    "city": "New York",
    "state": "NY",
    "postalCode": "10021"
  },
  "phoneNumber": [
    {
      "type": "home",
      "number": "212 555-1234"
    }, {
      "type": "fax",
      "number": "646 555-4567"
    }
  ]
});
```

String concatenation

For a language that deals with a lot of strings, JavaScript has always been pretty bad at building strings up from parts. Variables and expression values are often meant to be inserted inside a string somewhere, and this is usually done by concatenation using the `+` operator. If you've ever tried concatenating a couple of variables in a string, you'll know this soon becomes burdensome and hard to read.

CoffeeScript has a built-in string interpolation syntax, which is similar to many other scripting languages, but was specifically borrowed from Ruby. This is shown in the following code snippet:

CoffeeScript

```
greet = (name, time) ->
  "Good #{time} #{name}!"

alert (greet 'Pete', 'morning')
```

JavaScript

```
var greet;

greet = function(name, time) {
  return "Good " + time + " " +
name + "!";
};

alert(greet('Pete', 'morning'));
```

You can write any expression within `#{}` and its string value will be concatenated. Note that you can only use string interpolation in double-quoted strings, `""`. Single-quoted strings are literal and will be represented exactly how they are.

Equality

The equality operator `==` (and its inverse `!=`) in JavaScript is fraught with dangers, and a lot of times doesn't do what you would expect. This is because it will first try to coerce objects of a different type to be the same before comparing them.

It's also not transitive, meaning it might return different values of `true` or `false` depending on if a type is on the left or right of the operator. Please refer to the following code snippet:

```
'' == '0'           // false
0 == ''             // true
0 == '0'            // true

false == 'false'    // false
false == '0'        // true

false == undefined  // false
false == null       // false
null == undefined   // true
```

Because of its inconsistent and strange behavior, respected members in the JavaScript community advise avoiding it altogether and to rather use the identity operator, `===` in its place. This operator will always return `false` if two objects are of a different type, which is consistent to how `==` works in many other languages.

CoffeeScript will always convert `==` to `===` and `!=` to `!===`, as shown in the following implementation:

CoffeeScript	JavaScript
`'' == '0'`	`'' === '0';`
`0 == ''`	`0 === '';`
`0 == '0'`	`0 === '0';`
`false == 'false'`	`false === 'false';`
`false == '0'`	`false === '0';`
`false == undefined`	`false === void 0;`
`false == null`	`false === null;`
`null == undefined`	`null === void 0;`

The existential operator

When you're trying to check if a variable exists and has a value (is not `null` or `undefined`) in JavaScript, you need to use this quirky idiom:

```
typeof a !== "undefined" && a !== null
```

CoffeeScript has a nice shortcut for this, the existential operator `?`, which will return `false` unless a variable is `undefined` or `null`.

CoffeeScript

```
broccoli = true;
if carrots? && broccoli?
  alert 'this is healthy'
```

JavaScript

```
var broccoli;

broccoli = true;

if ((typeof carrots !==
"undefined" && carrots !== null)
&& (broccoli != null)) {
  alert('this is healthy');
}
```

In this example, since the compiler already knows that broccoli is defined, the `?` operator will only check if it has a `null` value, while it will check if `carrots` is `undefined` as well as `null`.

The existential operator has a method call variant: `?.` or just the "soak", which will allow you to swallow the method calls on `null` objects in a method chain, as shown here:

CoffeeScript	JavaScript

`street = person?.getAddress()?.street`	`var street, _ref;`
	
	`street = typeof person !== "undefined" && person !== null ? (_ref = person.getAddress()) != null ? _ref.street : void 0 : void 0;`

If all of the values in the chain exist, you should get the expected result. If any of them should be `null` or `undefined`, you will get an undefined value, instead of `TypeError` being thrown.

Although this is a powerful technique, it can also be easily abused and make the code hard to reason with. If you have long method chains it may become hard to know just exactly where the null or undefined value came from.

The **Law of Demeter**, a well-known object orientation design principle, can be used to minimize this kind of complexity and improve decoupling in your code. It can be summarized as follows:

- Your method can call other methods in its class directly
- Your method can call methods on its own fields directly (but not on the fields' fields)
- When your method takes parameters, your method can call methods on those parameters directly
- When your method creates local objects, that method can call methods on the local objects

Although, this is not a "strict law" in the sense that it should never be broken, it is more analogous to the law of nature, such that the code that tends to follow it also tends to be much simpler and more loosely coupled.

Now that we have spent some time going over some of the inadequacies and annoyances of JavaScript that CoffeeScript fixes, let's dwell on some of the other powerful features that CoffeeScript adds; some borrowed from other scripting languages and some that are unique to the language.

List comprehensions

In CoffeeScript, looping through collections works quite differently from JavaScript's imperative approach. CoffeeScript takes ideas from functional programming languages and uses list comprehensions to transform lists instead of looping through elements iteratively.

The while loop

The `while` loop is still present and works more or less the same, except that it can be used as an expression, meaning it will return an array of values:

CoffeeScript:

```
multiplesOf = (n, times) ->
  times++
  (n * times while times -= 1 > 0).reverse()

alert (multiplesOf 5, 10)
```

JavaScript:

```
var multiplesOf;

multiplesOf = function(n, times) {
  times++;
  return ((function() {
    var _results;
    _results = [];
    while (times -= 1 > 0) {
      _results.push(n * times);
    }
    return _results;
  })()).reverse();
};

alert(multiplesOf(5, 10));
```

Notice that in the previous code, the `while` body goes in front of the condition. This is a common idiom in CoffeeScript if the body is of only one line. You can do the same thing with `if` statements and list comprehensions.

We can improve the readability of the previous code slightly by using the `until` keyword, which is basically the negation of `while`, as shown here:

CoffeeScript:

```
multiplesOf = (n, times) ->
  times++
  (n * times until --times == 0).reverse()

alert (multiplesOf 5, 10)
```

JavaScript:

```
var multiplesOf;

multiplesOf = function(n, times) {
  times++;
  return ((function() {
    var _results;
    _results = [];
    while (--times !== 0) {
      _results.push(n * times);
    }
    return _results;
  })()).reverse();
};

alert(multiplesOf(5, 10));
```

The `for` statement doesn't work like it does in JavaScript. CoffeeScript replaces it with list comprehensions, which were mostly borrowed from the Python language and also very similar to constructs that you'll find in functional languages such as Haskell. Comprehensions provide a more declarative way of filtering, transforming, and aggregating collections or performing an action for each element. The best way to illustrate them would be through some examples:

CoffeeScript:

```
flavors = ['chocolate', 'strawberry', 'vanilla']
alert flavor for flavor in flavors

favorites = ("#{flavor}!" for flavor in flavors when flavor !=
'vanilla')
```

JavaScript:

```
var favorites, flavor, flavors, _i, _len;

flavors = ['chocolate', 'strawberry', 'vanilla'];

for (_i = 0, _len = flavors.length; _i < _len; _i++) {
  flavor = flavors[_i];
  alert(flavor);
}

favorites = (function() {
  var _j, _len1, _results;
  _results = [];
  for (_j = 0, _len1 = flavors.length; _j < _len1; _j++) {
    flavor = flavors[_j];
    if (flavor !== 'vanilla') {
      _results.push("" + flavor + "!");
    }
  }
  return _results;
})();
```

Although they are quite simple, comprehensions have a very condensed form and do a lot in very little code. Let's break it down to its separate parts:

```
[action or mapping] for [selector] in [collection] when [condition]
by [step]
```

Comprehensions are best read from right to left, starting from the `in` collection. The `selector` name is a temporary name that is given to each element as we iterate through the collection. The clause in front of the `for` keyword describes what you want to do with the `selector` name, by either calling a method with it as an argument, selecting a property or method on it, or assigning a value.

The `when` and `by` guard clauses are optional. They describe how the iteration should be filtered (elements will only be returned when their subsequent `when` condition is `true`), or which parts of the collection to select using `by` followed by a number. For example, `by 2` will return every evenly numbered element.

We can rewrite our `multiplesOf` function by using `by` and `when`:

CoffeeScript:

```
multiplesOf = (n, times) ->
  multiples = (m for m in [0..n*times] by n)
  multiples.shift()
  multiples

alert (multiplesOf 5, 10)
```

JavaScript:

```
var multiplesOf;

multiplesOf = function(n, times) {
  var m, multiples;
  multiples = (function() {
    var _i, _ref, _results;
    _results = [];
    for (m = _i = 0, _ref = n * times; 0 <= _ref ? _i <= _ref : _i >=
_ref; m = _i += n) {
      _results.push(m);
    }
    return _results;
  })();
  multiples.shift();
  return multiples;
};

alert(multiplesOf(5, 10));
```

The `[0..n*times]` syntax is CoffeeScripts's range syntax, which was borrowed from Ruby. It will create an array with all the elements between the first and last number. When the range has two dots it will be inclusive, meaning the range will contain the specified start and end element. If it has three dots (...), it will only contain the numbers in between.

List comprehensions were one of the biggest new concepts to grasp when I started learning CoffeeScript. They are an extremely powerful feature, but it does take some time to get used to and think in comprehensions. Whenever you feel tempted to write a looping construct using the lower level `while`, consider using a comprehension instead. They provide just about everything you could possibly need when working with collections, and they are extremely fast compared to built-in ECMAScript array methods, such as `.map()` and `.select()`.

You can use comprehensions to loop through key-value pairs in an object, using the `of` keyword, as shown in the following code:

CoffeeScript:

```
ages =
  john: 25
  peter: 26
  joan: 23

alert "#{name} is #{age} years old" for name, age of ages
```

JavaScript:

```
var age, ages, name;

ages = {
  john: 25,
  peter: 26,
  joan: 23
};

for (name in ages) {
  age = ages[name];
  alert("" + name + " is " + age + " years old");
}
```

Conditional clauses and logical aliases

CoffeeScript introduces some very nice logic and conditional features, some also borrowed from other scripting languages. The `unless` keyword is the inverse of the `if` keyword; `if` and `unless` can take the postfix form, meaning statements can go at the end of the line.

CoffeeScript also provides plain English aliases for some of the logical operators. They are as follows:

- `is` for `==`
- `isnt` for `!=`
- `not` for `!`
- `and` for `&&`

- `or` for `||`
- `true` can also be `yes`, or `on`
- `false` can be `no` or `off`

Putting all this together, let's look at some code to demonstrate it:

CoffeeScript:

```
car.switchOff() if car.ignition is on
service(car) unless car.lastService() > 15000
wash(car) if car.isDirty()
chargeFee(car.owner) if car.make isnt "Toyota"
```

JavaScript:

```
if (car.ignition === true) {
  car.switchOff();
}

if (!(car.lastService() > 15000)) {
  service(car);
}

if (car.isDirty()) {
  wash(car);
}

if (car.make !== "Toyota") {
  chargeFee(car.owner);
}
```

Array slicing and splicing

CoffeeScript allows you to easily extract parts of an array using the `..` and `...` notation. `[n..m]` will select all the elements including `n` and `m`, whereas `[n...m]` will select only the elements between `n` and `m`.

Both `[..]` and `[...]` will select the whole array. These are used in the following code:

CoffeeScript	JavaScript

`numbers = [0, 1, 2, 3, 4, 5, 6, 7, 8, 9]`
 	
`alert numbers[0..3]`
 	
`alert numbers[4...7]`
 	
`alert numbers[7..]`
 	
`alert numbers[..]`
	`var numbers;`
	
	`numbers = [0, 1, 2, 3, 4, 5, 6, 7, 8, 9];`
	
	`alert(numbers.slice(0, 4));`
	
	`alert(numbers.slice(4, 7));`
	
	`alert(numbers.slice(7));`
	
	`alert(numbers.slice(0));`

CoffeeScript sure loves its ellipses. They are used by splats, ranges, and array slices. Here are some quick tips on how to identify them: If the ... is next to the last argument in a function definition or a function call, it's a splat. If it's enclosed in square brackets that are not indexing an array, it's a range. If it is indexing an array, it's a slice.

Destructuring or pattern matching

Destructuring is a powerful concept that you'll find in many functional programming languages. In essence, it allows you to pull single values from complex objects. It can simply allow you to assign multiple values at once, or deal with functions that return multiple values; as shown here:

CoffeeScript:

```
getLocation = ->
  [
   'Chigaco'
   'Illinois'
   'USA'
  ]

[city, state, country] = getLocation()
```

JavaScript:

```
var city, country, getLocation, state, _ref;

getLocation = function() {
```

```
  return ['Chigaco', 'Illinois', 'USA'];
};

_ref = getLocation(), city = _ref[0], state = _ref[1], country = _
ref[2];
```

When you run this, you get three variables, `city`, `state`, and `country` with values that were assigned from the corresponding element in the array returned by the `getLocation` function.

You can use destructuring to pull out values from objects and hashes as well. There are no limits to how deeply data in the object can be nested. Here is an example of that:

CoffeeScript:

```
getAddress = ->
   address:
     country: 'USA'
     state: 'Illinois'
     city: 'Chicago'
     street: 'Rush Street'


{address: {street: myStreet}} = getAddress()
alert myStreet
```

JavaScript:

```
var getAddress, myStreet;

getAddress = function() {
  return {
    address: {
      country: 'USA',
      state: 'Illinois',
      city: 'Chicago',
      street: 'Rush Street'
    }
  };
};

myStreet = getAddress().address.street;

alert(myStreet);
```

In this example, the `{address: {street: ---}}` part describes your pattern, basically where to find the information you need. When we put the `myStreet` variable inside our pattern, we tell CoffeeScript to assign the value in that place to `myStreet`. While we can use nested objects, we can also mix and match destructuring objects and arrays, as shown in the following code:

CoffeeScript:

```
getAddress = ->
   address:
     country: 'USA'
     addressLines: [
       '1 Rush Street'
       'Chicago'
       'Illinois'
     ]

{address:
  {addressLines:
    [street, city, state]
  }
} = getAddress()
alert street
```

JavaScript:

```
var city, getAddress, state, street, _ref;

getAddress = function() {
  return {
    address: {
      country: 'USA',
      addressLines: ['1 Rush Street', 'Chicago', 'Illinois']
    }
  };
};

_ref = getAddress().address.addressLines, street = _ref[0], city =
_ref[1], state = _ref[2];

alert(street);
```

Here, in the previous code, we are pulling elements from the array value that we get from `addressLines` and give them names.

=> and @

In JavaScript, the value of `this` refers to the owner of the currently executing function, or the object that the function is a method of. Unlike in other object-oriented languages, JavaScript also has the notion that functions are not tightly bound to objects, meaning that the value of this can be changed at will (or accidently). This is a very powerful feature of the language but can also lead to confusion if used incorrectly.

In CoffeeScript, the `@` symbol is a shortcut for `this`. Whenever the compiler sees something like `@foo`, it will replace it with `this.foo`.

Although it's still possible to use this in CoffeeScript, it's generally frowned upon and more idiomatic to use `@` instead.

In any JavaScript function, the value of `this` is the object that the function is attached to. However, when you pass functions to other functions or reattach a function to another object, the value of `this` will change. Sometimes this is what you want, but often you would like to keep the original value of `this`.

For this purpose, CoffeeScript provides the `=>`, or fat arrow, which will define a function but at the same time capture the value of `this`, so that the function can be safely called in any context. This is especially useful when using callbacks, for instance in a jQuery event handler.

The following example will illustrate the idea:

CoffeeScript:

```
class Birthday
  prepare: (action) ->
    @action = action

  celebrate: () ->
   @action()

class Person
  constructor: (name) ->
    @name = name
    @birthday = new Birthday()
    @birthday.prepare () => "It's #{@name}'s birthday!"

michael = new Person "Michael"
alert michael.birthday.celebrate()
```

JavaScript:

```
var Birthday, Person, michael;

Birthday = (function() {

  function Birthday() {}

  Birthday.prototype.prepare = function(action) {
    return this.action = action;
  };

  Birthday.prototype.celebrate = function() {
    return this.action();
  };

  return Birthday;

})();

Person = (function() {

  function Person(name) {
    var _this = this;
    this.name = name;
    this.birthday = new Birthday();
    this.birthday.prepare(function() {
      return "It's " + _this.name + "'s birthday!";
    });
  }

  return Person;

})();

michael = new Person("Michael");

alert(michael.birthday.celebrate());
```

Notice that the `prepare` function on the `birthday` class takes an `action` function as an argument, to be called when the birthday occurs. Because we're passing this function using the fat arrow, it will have its scope fixed to the `Person` object. This means we can still refer to the `@name` instance variable even though it doesn't exist on the `Birthday` object that runs the function.

Switch statements

In CoffeeScript, `switch` statements take a different form, and look a lot less like JavaScript's Java-inspired syntax, and a lot more like Ruby's `case` statement. You don't need to call `break` to avoid falling through to the next `case` condition.

They have the following form:

```
switch condition
  when … then …
   ….
else …
```

Here, `else` is the default case.

Like everything else in CoffeeScript, they are expressions, and this can be assigned to a value.

Let's look at an example:

CoffeeScript:

```
languages = switch country
  when 'france' then 'french'
  when 'england', 'usa' then 'english'
  when 'belgium' then ['french', 'dutch']
  else 'swahili'
```

JavaScript:

```
var languages;

languages = (function() {
  switch (country) {
    case 'france':
      return 'french';
    case 'england':
    case 'usa':
      return 'english';
    case 'belgium':
      return ['french', 'dutch'];
    default:
      return 'swahili';
  }
})();
```

CoffeeScript doesn't force you to add a default `else` clause, although it is a good programming practice to always add one, just in case.

Chained comparisons

CoffeeScript borrowed chained comparisons from Python. These basically allow you to write greater than or less than comparisons like you would in mathematics, as shown here:

CoffeeScript	JavaScript

`age = 41`
 	
`alert 'middle age' if 61 > age > 39`
	`var age;`
	
	`age = 41;`
	
	`if ((61 > age && age > 39)) {`
	`  alert('middle age');`
	`}`

Block strings, block comments, and strings

Most programming books start with comments, and I thought I would end with them. In CoffeeScript, single line comments start with `#`. The comments do not end up in your generated output. Multiline comments start and end with `###`, and they are included in the generated JavaScript.

You can span a string over multiple lines using the `"""` triple quote to enclose it.

Summary

In this chapter, we started looking at CoffeeScript from JavaScript's perspective. We saw how it can help you write shorter, cleaner, and more elegant code than you normally would in JavaScript and avoid many of its pitfalls.

We came to realize that even though CoffeeScripts' syntax seems to be quite different from JavaScript, it actually maps pretty closely to its generated output.

Later on, we delved into some of CoffeeScripts' unique and wonderful additions, like list comprehensions, destructuring assignment, and its class syntax, as well as many more convenient and powerful features such as string interpolation, ranges, splats, and array slicing.

My goal in this chapter was to convince you that CoffeeScript is a superior alternative to JavaScript, and I have tried to do so by showing the differences between them. Although I have previously said "it's just JavaScript", I hope that you'll appreciate that CoffeeScript is a wonderful and modern language in its own right, with brilliant influences from other great scripting languages.

I can still write a great deal about the beauty of the language, but I feel that we have reached the point where we can dive into some real world CoffeeScript and get to appreciate it "in the wild", so to speak.

So, are you ready? Let's get started then and get CoffeeScript installed.

2
Running CoffeeScript

In this chapter, we'll talk about getting CoffeeScript installed and running on your development environment.

CoffeeScript can easily be installed on a Mac, Windows, or Linux. There are a variety of ways by which you can get it running, depending on if you just want the install to be simple and straightforward or if you want to be on the bleeding edge. Before we start on the details though, it's good to know that CoffeeScript usually doesn't live on its own, and uses some great JavaScript tools and frameworks to do its magic. Let's briefly discuss the typical CoffeeScript stack.

The CoffeeScript stack

Early on in CoffeeScript's history, its compiler was written in Ruby. Later on, it became self-hosting; the language compiler was written in itself. This means that the compiler for CoffeeScript was written in CoffeeScript code which could then be compiled to JavaScript, which could then be run to compile CoffeeScript again. Confusing, isn't it?

Without going any further into what a feat this is, this also means that in order to run CoffeeScript, we need to be able to execute JavaScript standalone on your computer, without a browser.

Node.js, or just **Node**, is a JavaScript framework designed for writing network-server applications. It's built using Google's V8, an engine that can run JavaScript without a web browser—a perfect fit for CoffeeScript. It has become the preferred way to install CoffeeScript.

Pairing CoffeeScript with Node.js has a lot of benefits. Not only does this mean that you can compile JavaScript that can be run in a browser, but you also get a full-fledged JavaScript network application server framework with hundreds of useful libraries that have been written for it.

As with JavaScript in Node.js, you can write and execute CoffeeScript on the server, use it to write web server applications and even use it as a normal, everyday systems scripting language.

> The core CoffeeScript compiler has no dependencies to Node and can technically be executed on any JavaScript environment. However, the coffee command-line utility that uses the compiler is a Node.js package.

The working of the CoffeeScript compiler is shown in the following diagram:

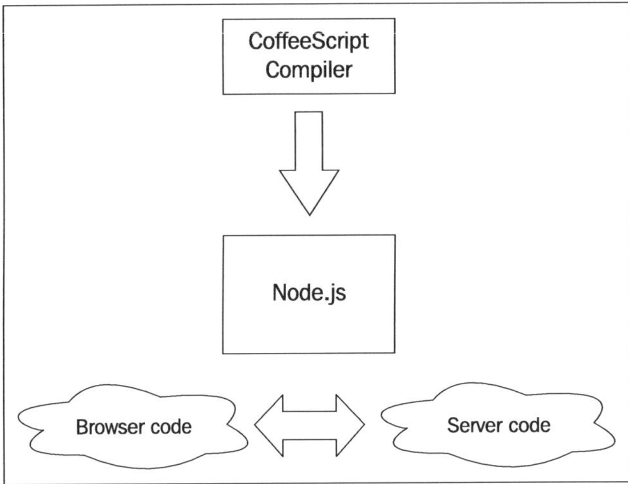

Node.js and npm

Node.js has its own package management system, called **npm**. It's used to install and manage packages, libraries, and their dependencies that run in the Node.js ecosystem. It is also the most common way of installing CoffeeScript, which itself is available as an npm package. Thus, it's actually very easy to install CoffeeScript after you have set up Node.js and npm.

There are different ways of installing Node.js and npm, depending on your Operating System and if you need to compile the source or not. Each of the subsequent sections will cover the instructions for your OS.

The Node.js wiki contains a ton of information on installing and running Node on a plethora of platforms. If you run into any trouble during this chapter, you can look at it, since it has a lot of tips on troubleshooting issues and is updated often; the link is `https://github.com/joyent/node/wiki/Installation`.

Node.js, npm, and CoffeeScript on Windows

There has been a great drive within the Node.js community for good native Windows support and it is very easy to install.

To do so, first head on over to the Node.js website (`nodejs.org`) and then click on the **Downloads** button. You'll see a couple of options available, but choose the **Windows Installer** option, which is shown in the following screenshot:

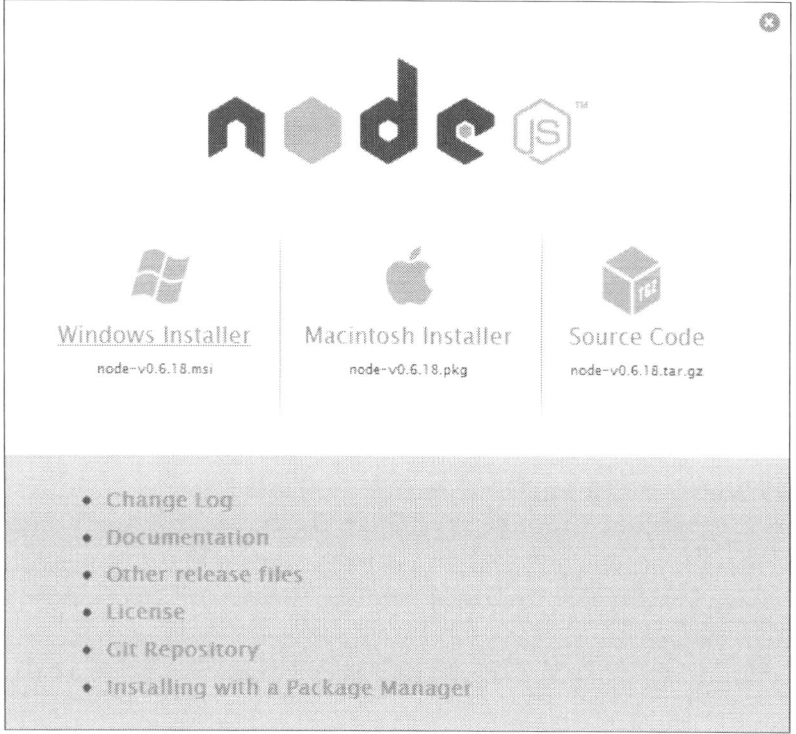

This will download an `.msi` file. Once you have downloaded it, running the install couldn't be much easier; just accept the terms and click on **Continue**. If you see the following screen, then you have successfully installed Node:

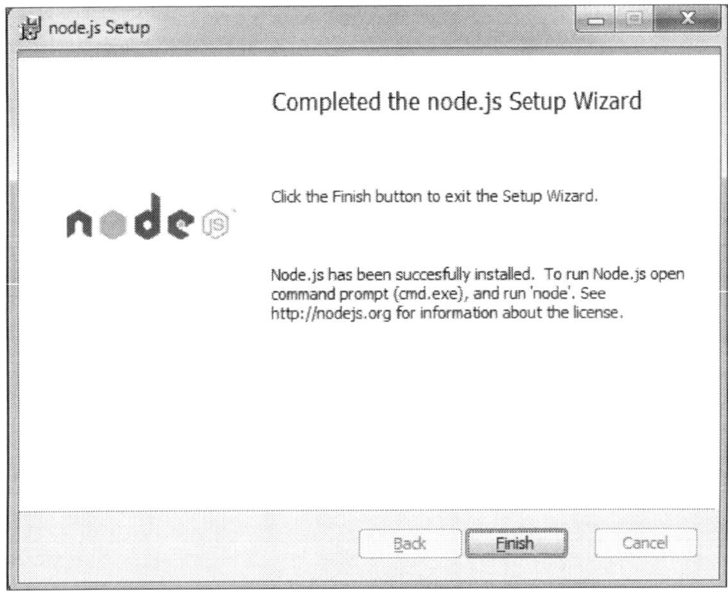

At this point, you might need to log out of Windows or restart so that changes to your `$PATH` variables can take effect. After you have done this, you should be able to open the DOS command prompt and run the following:

```
node -v
```

This should spit out a version, which means you're good to go. Let's also check if npm is working fine. Also in the command-line tool, enter the following:

```
npm
```

You should see something similar to the following screenshot:

```
C:\Users\michael>npm

Usage: npm <command>

where <command> is one of:
    add-user, adduser, apihelp, author, bin, bugs, c, cache,
    completion, config, deprecate, docs, edit, explore, faq,
    find, get, help, help-search, home, i, info, init, install,
    la, link, list, ll, ln, login, ls, outdated, owner, pack,
    prefix, prune, publish, r, rb, rebuild, remove, restart, rm,
    root, run-script, s, se, search, set, show, shrinkwrap,
    star, start, stop, submodule, tag, test, un, uninstall,
    unlink, unpublish, unstar, up, update, version, view,
    whoami

npm <cmd> -h     quick help on <cmd>
npm -l           display full usage info
npm faq          commonly asked questions
npm help <term>  search for help on <term>
npm help npm     involved overview

Specify configs in the ini-formatted file:
    C:\Users\michael\.npmrc
or on the command line via: npm <command> --key value
Config info can be viewed via: npm help config

npm@1.1.21 C:\Program Files (x86)\nodejs\node_modules\npm

C:\Users\michael>
```

Now, in order to go ahead and install CoffeeScript, just enter the following command:

```
npm install coffee-script
```

If all went well, you should see something similar to the following screenshot:

```
C:\Users\michael>npm install -g coffee-script
npm http GET https://registry.npmjs.org/coffee-script
npm http 200 https://registry.npmjs.org/coffee-script
npm http GET https://registry.npmjs.org/coffee-script/-/coffee-script-1.3.3.tgz
npm http 200 https://registry.npmjs.org/coffee-script/-/coffee-script-1.3.3.tgz
C:\Users\michael\AppData\Roaming\npm\coffee -> C:\Users\michael\AppData\Roaming\
npm\node_modules\coffee-script\bin\coffee
C:\Users\michael\AppData\Roaming\npm\cake -> C:\Users\michael\AppData\Roaming\np
m\node_modules\coffee-script\bin\cake
coffee-script@1.3.3 C:\Users\michael\AppData\Roaming\npm\node_modules\coffee-scr
ipt

C:\Users\michael>
```

Here, I used the **-g** flag, which installs the npm package for all users. Once you have installed CoffeeScript, we can test it using the **coffee** command, as shown here:

```
C:\Users\michael>coffee
coffee> 1 + 1
2
coffee>
```

This is the CoffeeScript interpreter, and as you can see, you can use it to run CoffeeScript code on the fly. To exit, just use *Ctrl* + *C*.

And that's it! Installing Node.js on Windows is really quick and easy.

Installing CoffeeScript on a Mac

There are two ways of installing Node.js on a Mac, either by downloading the `.pkg` file from the Node.js website and installing it using Apple's installer application, or by using the **Homebrew** command-line package manager.

The easiest way of getting up and running is by just installing the `.pkg` file, so let's go over that first. Installing Homebrew might involve more work, but it is worth it if you prefer working on the command-line tool and would build CoffeeScript from source.

Using the Apple installer

Head on over to the Node.js website (`nodejs.org`) and then click on the **Downloads** button. You'll see a couple of options available, but choose the **Macintosh Installer** option, as shown in the following screenshot:

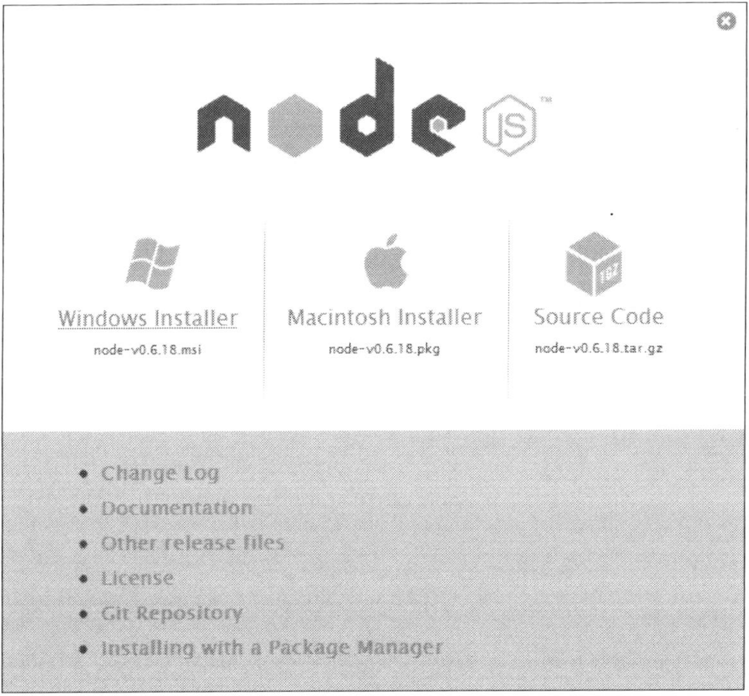

This will download a `.pkg` file. Once you have downloaded it, running the install couldn't be much easier; just choose your destination, accept the license, and click **Continue**. You should choose to install it for all users by using the **Install for all users of this computer** option, which is shown in the following screenshot:

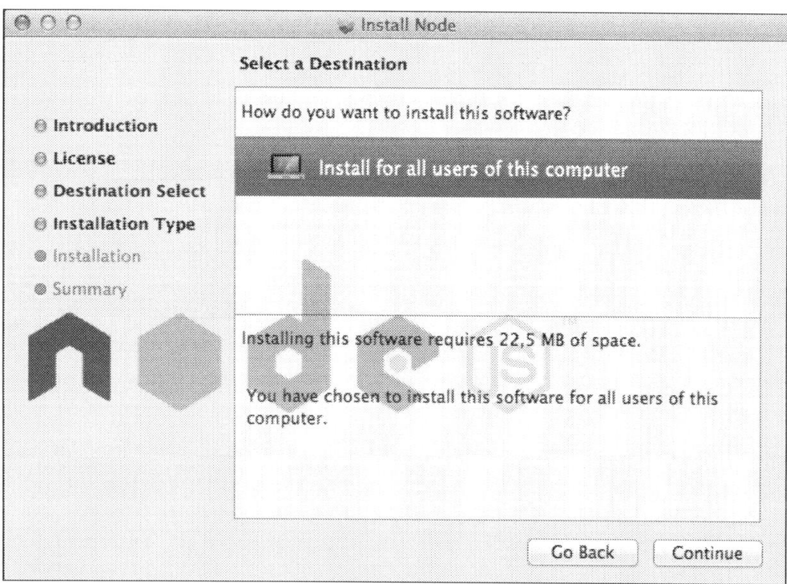

If you see the following screen, then you have successfully installed Node:

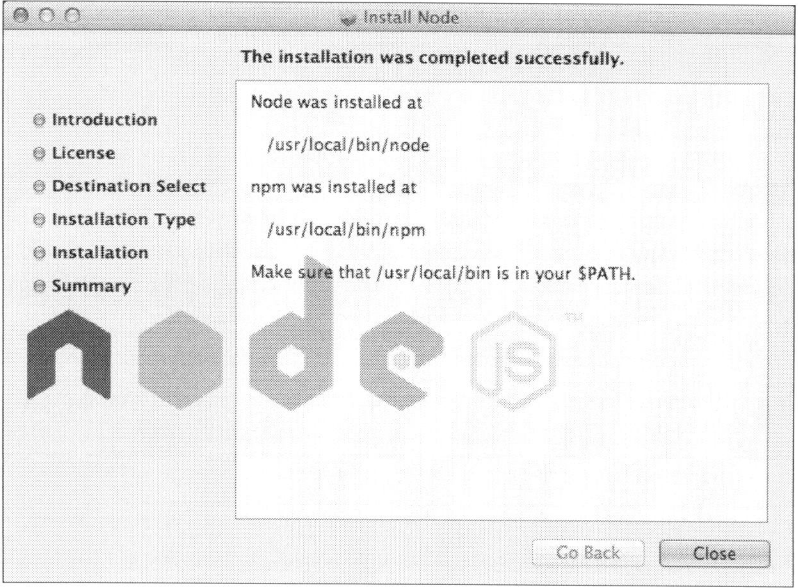

You will also have npm installed, which we'll use to install CoffeeScript. Skip to the *Installing CoffeeScript with npm* section.

Using Homebrew

A lot of developers prefer working on the command-line tool on a Mac, and the Homebrew package manager has become quite popular. It aims to let you easily install Unix tools that don't come with Mac OS X.

If you prefer installing Node.js using Homebrew, you need to have Homebrew on your system. You might also need to have XCode command-line tools to build the Node.js source code. The Homebrew wiki contains instructions on how to get it up and running at `https://github.com/mxcl/homebrew/wiki/installation`.

If you do have Homebrew installed, you can then install Node.js using the **brew** command, as shown in the following screenshot:

```
$  brew install node
==> Downloading http://nodejs.org/dist/v0.6.13/node-v0.6.13.tar.gz
######################################################################## 100.0%
==> ./configure --prefix=/usr/local/Cellar/node/0.6.13 --without-npm
==> make install
==> Caveats
Homebrew has NOT installed npm. We recommend the following method of
installation:
  curl http://npmjs.org/install.sh | sh

After installing, add the following path to your NODE_PATH environment
variable to have npm libraries picked up:
  /usr/local/lib/node_modules
==> Summary
/usr/local/Cellar/node/0.6.13: 80 files, 7.4M, built in 3.7 minutes
$
```

As you can see from the output, Homebrew has not installed npm, without which we cannot install CoffeeScript. To install npm, you can just copy and paste the following command in the terminal:

```
curl http://npmjs.org/install.sh |sh
```

After npm is installed, you should see something similar to the following screen:

```
$  curl http://npmjs.org/install.sh | sh
  % Total    % Received % Xferd  Average Speed   Time    Time     Time  Current
                                 Dload  Upload   Total   Spent    Left  Speed
100  7881  100  7881    0     0   7507      0  0:00:01  0:00:01 --:--:-- 13267
tar=/usr/bin/tar
version:
bsdtar 2.8.3 - libarchive 2.8.3
install npm@1.1
fetching: http://registry.npmjs.org/npm/-/npm-1.1.23.tgz
0.6.13
1.1.23
cleanup prefix=/usr/local

All clean!

> npm@1.1.23 prepublish .
> npm prune; rm -rf node_modules/*/{test,example,bench}*; make -j4 doc

sh: npm: command not found
make: Nothing to be done for `doc'.
/usr/local/bin/npm -> /usr/local/lib/node_modules/npm/bin/npm-cli.js
npm@1.1.23 /usr/local/lib/node_modules/npm
It worked
$
```

Installing CoffeeScript with npm

Now that we have npm installed, we should be able to install CoffeeScript. Just enter the following command in the terminal:

```
npm install -g coffee-script
```

The **-g** flag lets npm install CoffeeScript globally; once this is done, you can now test if CoffeeScript is working by using the **coffee** command, as shown in the following screenshot:

```
$  npm install -g coffee-script
npm http GET https://registry.npmjs.org/coffee-script
npm http 200 https://registry.npmjs.org/coffee-script
npm http GET https://registry.npmjs.org/coffee-script/-/coffee-script-1.3.3.tgz
npm http 200 https://registry.npmjs.org/coffee-script/-/coffee-script-1.3.3.tgz
/usr/local/bin/coffee -> /usr/local/lib/node_modules/coffee-script/bin/coffee
/usr/local/bin/cake -> /usr/local/lib/node_modules/coffee-script/bin/cake
coffee-script@1.3.3 /usr/local/lib/node_modules/coffee-script
$  coffee -v
CoffeeScript version 1.3.3
$
```

And that's it! Installing CoffeeScript on a Mac is quite easy.

Installing CoffeeScript on Linux

The ways of installing Node.js with CoffeeScript on Linux vary depending on which distribution you have installed. There are packages for most of the popular distros, and if not, you can also try building CoffeeScript from a source, as described in the next section.

I only have experience with package managers for Debian-based distros and have installed CoffeeScript with Node.js successfully using the **apt-get** package manager. However, you should be able to follow the instructions for the other distros as described.

There are apt-get packages for Node.js on Ubuntu, MintOS, and Debian, but you need to add sources for them before you can install. The instructions for installing each of them will be explored in the following sections.

Ubuntu and MintOS

Enter the following on the command-line utility (you might need to have sufficient permissions to use `sudo`):

```
sudo apt-get install python-software-properties
sudo apt-add-repository ppa:chris-lea/node.js
sudo apt-get update
sudo apt-get install nodejs npm
```

Debian

On Debian, you would normally log in to a root terminal to install packages. Once logged in, enter the following command:

```
echo deb http://ftp.us.debian.org/debian/ sid main > /etc/apt/sources.
list.d/sid.list
apt-get update
apt-get install nodejs npm
```

Other distributions

The Node.js wiki page at `https://github.com/joyent/node/wiki/Installing-Node.js-via-package-manager` contains instructions for installing on a variety of Linux and Unix distributions, including Fedora, openSUSE, Arch Linux, and FreeDSB.

Installing CoffeeScript with npm

After your package manager has done its thing, you should now have Node.js and npm installed. You can verify this by using the npm **-v** command. You can now install CoffeeScript using npm by entering the following command:

```
npm install -g coffee-script
```

The `-g` flag tells npm to install the package globally.

The following screenshot shows how the **-v** command is used to install CoffeeScript:

```
root@octopus:/home/michael# npm -v
1.1.4
root@octopus:/home/michael# npm install -g coffee-script
npm http GET https://registry.npmjs.org/coffee-script
npm http 304 https://registry.npmjs.org/coffee-script
/usr/local/bin/coffee -> /usr/local/lib/node_modules/coffee-script/bin/coffee
/usr/local/bin/cake -> /usr/local/lib/node_modules/coffee-script/bin/cake
coffee-script@1.3.3 /usr/local/lib/node_modules/coffee-script
root@octopus:/home/michael# coffee -v
CoffeeScript version 1.3.3
root@octopus:/home/michael#
```

And that's it! Installing CoffeeScript on Linux is quite easy.

Building Node.js from source

If you prefer not to use a package manager or installer, or don't have one available for your OS, or you would like to get the very latest version of Node.js, then you can also build Node.js from its source. Be warned though, this process is often fraught with danger, since the source often needs some dependencies on the system to build.

Building on Linux or Unix

To build on a Linux or Unix environment, you need to make sure that you have the following source dependencies installed:

- **Python-Version 2.6 or Version 2.7**: You can check if you have Python installed and also check which version is installed by entering `python --version` in the command prompt.
- **libssl-dev**: This can usually be installed with the built-in package manager. It's already installed on OS X.

I'm going to show you how to build Node.js using its latest source. The source is managed using the popular Git version control system and hosted in a repository on `github.com`. To pull the latest source from your github, you'll need to make sure you have Git installed. By using `apt-get`, you can install it as such:

```
apt-get install git-core
```

Once you have these prerequisites, you should be able to build the node. Enter the following command on the command-line tool:

```
git clone https://github.com/joyent/node.git
cd node
git checkout v0.6.19
./configure
make
sudo make install
```

Phew! If everything went well, you should be able to install CoffeeScript using npm:

```
npm install -g coffee-script
```

Building on Windows

Although it's possible to build Node.js on Windows, I would highly recommend that you just run the installer instead. Out of all the ways of installing that I have mentioned in this book, this is the only one I didn't do myself. This example comes straight from the Node wiki (`https://github.com/joyent/node/wiki/Installation`). Apparently, the build can take a very long time. In the command prompt, enter the following:

```
C:\Users\ryan>tar -zxf node-v0.6.5.tar.gz
C:\Users\ryan>cd node-v0.6.5
C:\Users\ryan\node-v0.6.5>vcbuild.bat release
C:\Users\ryan\node-v0.6.5>Release\node.exe
> process.versions
{ node: '0.6.5',
  v8: '3.6.6.11',
  ares: '1.7.5-DEV',
  uv: '0.6',
  openssl: '0.9.8r' }
>
```

Using CoffeeScript

And there you have it. Having to install Node.js and npm just to get CoffeeScript might seem like a lot of effort, but you'll get to experience the power of having a wonderful server-side JavaScript framework and good command-line tools to write CoffeeScript with.

Now that you have CoffeeScript installed, how do we go about using it? Your main entry point into the language is the `coffee` command.

The coffee command

This command-line utility is like a Swiss army knife of CoffeeScript. You can use it to run CoffeeScript in an interactive fashion, compile CoffeeScript files into JavaScript files, execute `.coffee` files, watch files or directories, and compile if any of the files change, as well as a few other useful things. Executing the command is easy, just enter `coffee` along with some options and arguments for them.

For help on all the available options, run `coffee` with the **-h** or **--help** options. A list of useful options are shown in the following screenshot:

```
C:\Users\michael>coffee -h

Usage: coffee [options] path/to/script.coffee -- [args]

If called without options, `coffee` will run your script.

  -b, --bare          compile without a top-level function wrapper
  -c, --compile       compile to JavaScript and save as .js files
  -e, --eval          pass a string from the command line as input
  -h, --help          display this help message
  -i, --interactive   run an interactive CoffeeScript REPL
  -j, --join          concatenate the source CoffeeScript before compiling
  -l, --lint          pipe the compiled JavaScript through JavaScript Lint
  -n, --nodes         print out the parse tree that the parser produces
      --nodejs        pass options directly to the "node" binary
  -o, --output        set the output directory for compiled JavaScript
  -p, --print         print out the compiled JavaScript
  -r, --require       require a library before executing your script
  -s, --stdio         listen for and compile scripts over stdio
  -t, --tokens        print out the tokens that the lexer/rewriter produce
  -v, --version       display the version number
  -w, --watch         watch scripts for changes and rerun commands
```

We have already seen the **-v** option, which will print out the current version of CoffeeScript.

The REPL

Executing `coffee` with no arguments or the **-i** option will drop you into the CoffeeScript **Read Eval Print Loop (REPL)**. From here, you can type in CoffeeScript code that will be executed on the fly and display its output right in the console. This is very useful for playing with the language, exploring some of the core JavaScript and Node.js libraries, or even pulling in another external library or API and being able to explore it interactively.

I urge you to run the coffee REPL and try some of the code examples that we discussed in the previous chapter. Notice how the output of each expression is displayed after it is entered. The interpreter is also clever enough to handle multiline and nested expressions, such as function definitions.

```
michael@walrus ~ $ coffee
coffee> 1 + 1
2
coffee> greet = -> "Hello"
[Function]
coffee> greet()
'Hello'
coffee>
```

In the previous screenshot, the interpreter is shown handling a function definition.

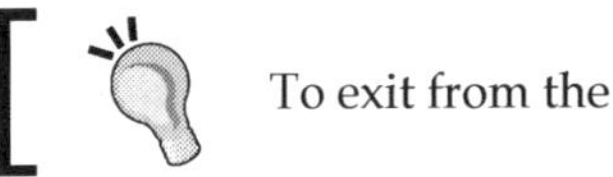

To exit from the REPL, use *Ctrl* + *D* or *Ctrl* + *C*.

Running .coffee files

After typing enough code into the REPL, you will come to a point when you will want to start storing and organizing your CoffeeScript in source files. CoffeeScript files use the `.coffee` extension. You can run a `.coffee` file by passing it as an argument to the `coffee` command. The CoffeeScript in the file will be compiled to JavaScript and then executed, using Node.js as its environment.

You can use any text editor to write your CoffeeScript. A lot of popular editors have plugins or have added support for CoffeeScript, with features such as syntax highlighting, code completion, or even allowing you to run your code right from the editor. There is a comprehensive list of text editors and plugins that support CoffeeScript at `https://github.com/jashkenas/coffee-script/wiki/Text-editor-plugins`.

Compiling to JavaScript

To compile a CoffeeScript to JavaScript, we pass the **-c** or **--compile** option. It takes either a single argument with a filename or a folder name, or multiple files and folder names. If you specify a folder, it will compile all the files in that folder. By default, the JavaScript output files will have the same name as the source file, so `foo.coffee` will compile to `foo.js`.

If we wanted to control where the outputted JavaScript will be written, then we can use the **-o** or **--output** option with a folder name. If you're specifying multiple files or folders, then you can also pass the **-j** or **--join** option with a filename. This will join the output into a single JavaScript file.

Watching

If you're developing a CoffeeScript application, it can become tedious to keep running **--compile**. Another useful option is **-w** or **--watch**. This tells the CoffeeScript compiler to keep running and watch a certain file or folder for any changes to the files. This works well when combined with **--compile**, which will compile files every time they change.

Putting it all together

The cool thing about the `coffee` command is that the flags can be combined to create a very useful build and development environment. Let's say, I have a bunch of CoffeeScript files in a source folder that I want to compile to a single `output.js` file in the `js` folder every time a file changes.

You should be able to use something similar to the following command:

```
coffee -o js/ -j output.js -cw source/
```

This will watch for any changes to the `.coffee` files in the source folder and compile and join them into a single file called **output.js** inside the **js** folder, as shown in the following screenshot:

```
michael@walrus ~ $ coffee -o js/ -j output.js -cw source/
22:29:01 - compiled output.js
22:29:10 - compiled output.js
```

Summary

In this chapter, you have hopefully learned how to get CoffeeScript running on the development environment of your choice. You have also learned how to use the `coffee` command to run and compile CoffeeScript. Now that you have the tools, we'll move to writing some code and get to know CoffeeScript "in the wild", so to speak. Let's start from where JavaScript started, and look at programming CoffeeScript in the browser.

3

CoffeeScript and jQuery

jQuery is a cross-browser compatible library designed to simplify the life of an HTML application developer. It was first released by John Resig in 2006 and has since become the most popular JavaScript library in the world, and is used in millions of websites.

Why did it become so popular? Well, jQuery has a couple of nice features like easy DOM manipulation and querying, event handling, and animation, as well as AJAX support. All these combined together makes programming against the DOM and programming in JavaScript much better.

The library has also been highly optimized in terms of cross-browser compatibility and speed and thus using jQuery's DOM traversal and manipulation functions not only save you from writing tedious code, but it's also usually much faster than the code that you could write yourself.

As it turns out, jQuery and CoffeeScript go very well together, and when combined, provides a powerful toolset to write web applications in a succinct and expressive manner.

In this chapter, we'll do the following:

- Explore some of the high level features of jQuery and talk about what it gives you
- Learn how to use CoffeeScript and jQuery in the browser
- Build a simple to-do list app using jQuery and CoffeeScript

Let's start by discussing the jQuery library in more detail, and discover what makes it so useful.

Finding and changing elements

In web browsers, the DOM, or Document Object Model, is the representation of the elements in an HTML document used to interact with programmatically.

In JavaScript, you'll find yourself doing a lot of DOM traversal to find elements that you're interested in and then manipulate them.

To accomplish this using just the standard JavaScript libraries, you'll usually need to use a combination of the `document.getElementsByName`, `document.getElementById`, and `document.getElementsById` methods. As soon as your HTML structure starts getting complex, this usually means that you would have to combine these methods in an awkward and cumbersome iteration code.

Code written in this fashion usually makes a lot of assumptions about the structure of your HTML, which means that it will usually break if the HTML changes.

The $ function

With jQuery, a lot of this imperative style code becomes much simpler with the `$` function—jQuery's factory method (a method that creates instances of jQuery classes) and the entry point into most of the library.

This function usually takes a CSS selector string as an argument, which can be used to select one or multiple elements according to their element name, ID, class attribute, or other attribute values. This method will return a jQuery object that contains one or more elements that matches the selector.

Here, we'll select all the `input` tags in a document with a class of `address`, using the `$` function:

```
$('input .address')
```

You can then manipulate or interrogate these elements using a multitude of functions, often called **commands**. The following are just a few of the common jQuery commands and what they are used for:

- `addClass`: This adds a CSS class to an element
- `removeClass`: This removes a CSS class from an element
- `attr`: This gets a attribute from an element
- `hasClass`: This checks for the existence of a CSS class on an element
- `html`: This gets or sets the HTML text of an element
- `val`: This gets or sets the element value

- `show`: This displays an element
- `hide`: This hides an element
- `parent`: This gets the parent of an element
- `appendTo`: This appends a child element
- `fadeIn`: This fades in an element
- `fadeout`: This fades out an element

Most of the commands return a jQuery object that can be used to chain other commands onto them. By chaining commands, you can use the output of one command as the input of the next. This powerful technique lets you write very short and succinct transformations on parts of the HTML document.

Let's say that we want to highlight and enable all the `address` inputs in an HTML form; jQuery allows us to do something similar to this:

```
$('input .address').addClass('highlighted').removeAttr('disabled')
```

Here, we once again select all the `input` tags with an `address` class. We add the `highlighted` class to each using the `addClass` command, and then remove the `disabled` attribute by chaining a call to the `removeAttr` command.

Utility functions

jQuery also comes with a host of utility functions that generally improves your day-to-day JavaScript programming experience. These are all in the form of methods on the global jQuery object like this: `$.methodName`. For instance, one of the most widely used utilities is the `each` method, that can be used to iterate over arrays or objects, and would be called as follows (in CoffeeScript):

```
$.each [1, 2, 3, 4], (index, value) -> alert(index + ' is ' + value)
```

jQuery's utility methods range from array and collection helper methods, time and string manipulation, as well as a host of other useful JavaScript and browser related functions. A lot of these functions stem from the everyday needs of a lot of JavaScript programmers.

Often, you'll find a function that applies to a common problem or pattern you face yourself when writing JavaScript or CoffeeScript. You can find a detailed list of the functions at `http://api.jquery.com/category/utilities/`.

Ajax methods

jQuery provides the `$.ajax` method to perform Ajax requests that work across browsers. Traditionally, this has been a pain to do, since browsers all implemented different interfaces for handling Ajax. jQuery takes care of all of that and provides a simpler, callback-based way of constructing and executing Ajax requests. This means that you can declaratively specify how the Ajax call should be made and then provide functions that jQuery will call back when the request succeeds or fails.

Using jQuery

Using jQuery in the browser is very simple; you just need to include the jQuery library in your HTML file. You can either download the latest version of jQuery from their site (`http://docs.jquery.com/Downloading_jQuery`) and reference that, or you can directly link to a **Content Delivery Network** (**CDN**) version of the library.

Following is an example of how you might do it. This snippet comes from the excellent HTML5 Boilerplate project (`http://html5boilerplate.com/`). Here we include the latest minified jQuery from a Google CDN, but we will also include a local version if including from the CDN fails.

```
<script src="//ajax.googleapis.com/ajax/libs/jquery/1.7.2/jquery.min.
js"></script>
    <script>window.jQuery || document.write('<script src="js/lib/
jquery-1.7.2.min.js"><\/script>')
</script>
```

Using CoffeeScript and jQuery in the browser

Before we can start playing with jQuery and CoffeeScript, let's talk about how you go about writing CoffeeScript code that runs in the browser.

Compiling CoffeeScript

The most common way of compiling CoffeeScript for a web application is to run the `coffee` command to watch one or more CoffeeScript files for changes and then to compile them to JavaScript. The output will then be included in your web application.

As an example, we'll organize our project folder structure to look something like the following folder structure:

The **src** folder is where your CoffeeScript files would go. We could then start a CoffeeScript compiler to watch that folder and compile the JavaScript to our **public/js** folder.

This is what the CoffeeScript command would look like:

```
coffee -co public/js -w src/
```

Keep this command running in the background in its own terminal window and it will recompile your CoffeeScript files when you save them.

CoffeeScript tags

Another way of running CoffeeScript in the browser is to include CoffeeScript inline in the document enclosed in the <script type="text/coffeescript"> tag and then to include the minified CoffeeScript compiler script (`coffee-script.js`) in your document. This will compile, and then run all the inline CoffeeScript in the page.

This isn't meant for serious use, since you will pay a serious performance penalty for the compiling step each time the page is loaded. However, it can be quite useful from time to time to just quickly play around with some CoffeeScript in the browser without setting up a complete compiler chain.

jQuery and CoffeeScript

Let's put something in our CoffeeScript file to see if we can successfully hook it up with jQuery. In the `src` folder, create a file named `app.coffee` and include the following code:

```
$ -> alert "It works!"
```

This sets up the jQuery's `$(document).ready()` function that will be called when the application is initialized. Here we are using the shorthand syntax for it, by just passing an anonymous function to the `$` function.

You should now have an `app.js` file in the `public/js` folder with content similar to this:

```
// Generated by CoffeeScript 1.3.3
(function() {
    alert('It works!');
}).call(this);
```

Lastly, we need to include this file as well as the jQuery in our application's HTML file. In the `public/index.html` file, add the following code:

```
<!doctype html>
<html lang="en">
<head>
  <meta charset="utf-8">
  <meta http-equiv="X-UA-Compatible" content="IE=edge,chrome=1">
  <title>jQuery and CoffeeScript Todo</title>
  <link rel="stylesheet" href="css/styles.css">
</head>
<body>
  <script src="http://ajax.googleapis.com/ajax/libs/jquery/1.7.2/
jquery.min.js"></script>
  <script src="js/app.js"></script>
</body>
</html>
```

The preceding code creates our HTML skeleton, and includes jQuery (using the Google CDN) as well as our application code.

Downloading the example code

You can download the example code files for all Packt books you have purchased from your account at `http://www.PacktPub.com`. If you purchased this book elsewhere, you can visit `http://www.PacktPub.com/` support and register to have the files e-mailed directly to you.

Testing it all

We should now be able to run our application by opening our `index.html` file in a browser. If all went well, we should see our alert pop-up window, as shown in the following screenshot:

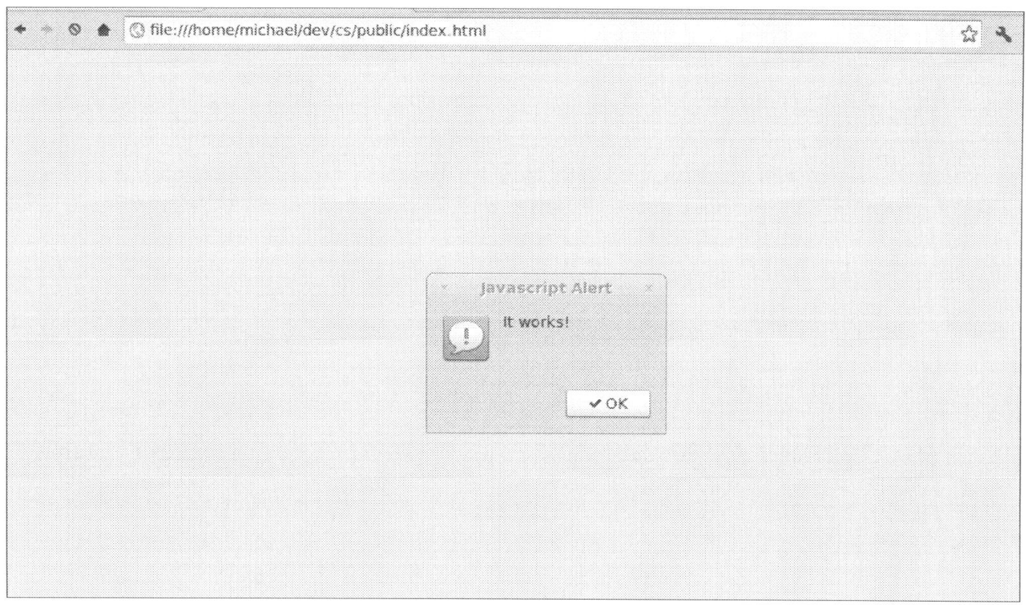

Running a local web server

While we can easily test our web application from the disk for now, we might want to host it on a local web server soon, especially if we wanted to start doing Ajax. Since we already have Node.js installed, it should be really easy to run a web server, for which we only need to serve static content for now. Luckily, there is an npm package that will do just that for us; it is named **http-server** and can be found at `https://github.com/nodeapps/http-server`.

To install it, just run the following command:

```
npm install http-server -g
```

And then, we execute it by navigating to our application folder and entering this:

```
http-server
```

This will host all the files in the public folder on port **8080**. We should now be able to navigate to our hosted site by using the URL `http://localhost:8080/`.

Our application

In the rest of this chapter, we will be building a jQuery application using CoffeeScript. The application is a to-do list app, which can be used to keep track of your daily tasks and how you completed them.

TodoMVC

I have modeled a lot of the application on some of the TodoMVC project's source code, which is in the public domain. This project is a showcase of different JavaScript MVC frameworks all used to build the same application, and can be very useful when evaluating frameworks. If you wanted to check it out, it can be found at `http://addyosmani.github.com/todomvc/`.

MVC, or Model-view-controller, is a widely used application architecture pattern that aims to simplify code and reduce coupling by splitting application concerns into three domain object types. We'll talk about MVC a bit more later on in the book.

We will mostly base our application on the TodoMVC project to get the awesome-looking stylesheets that come with it as well as a well-designed HTML5 structure. However, most of the client-side JavaScript will be rewritten in CoffeeScript and it will be simplified and modified quite a lot for illustration purposes.

So without further ado, let's get to it!

Our initial HTML

First, we'll add some HTML that will allow us to enter to-do items and view a list of existing items. In `index.html`, add the following code to the `body` tag, right before the included `script` tags:

```
<section id="todoapp">
    <header id="header">
      <h1>todos</h1>
      <input id="new-todo" placeholder="What needs to be done?"
autofocus>
    </header>
    <section id="main">
      <ul id="todo-list"></ul>
    </section>
    <footer id="footer">
      <button id="clear-completed">Clear completed</button>
    </footer>
  </section>
```

Let's briefly walk through the structure of the preceding markup. First, we have a section with the `todoapp` ID, that will serve as the main part of the app. It consists of a `header` tag, which will house our input for creating new items, a `main` section, which will list all our to-do items, and a `footer` section that will have the **Clear completed** button. Before we open this page in the browser, let's remove the previous alert line from our `app.coffee` file.

When you navigate to this page, it won't look like much. That is because our HTML hasn't been styled at all. Download the `styles.css` file for this chapter and copy it to the `public/css` folder. It should now look much better.

Initializing our app

Most jQuery apps, including ours, follow a similar pattern. We create a `$(document).ready` handler which in turn performs page initialization, usually including hooking up event handlers for user actions. Let's do this in our `app.coffee` file.

```
class TodoApp
  constructor: ->
    @bindEvents()

  bindEvents: ->
    alert 'binding events'


$ ->
  app = new TodoApp()
```

Here, in the previous code snippet, we create a class called `TodoApp` that will represent our application. It has a constructor that calls the `bindEvents` method, which for now just displays an alert message.

We set up jQuery's `$(document).ready` event handler to create an instance of our `TodoApp`. When you reload the page, you should see the **binding events** alert pop-up window.

> **Not seeing the expected output?**
>
> Remember to keep an eye on the output of the coffee compiler running in the background. If you have made any syntax errors, then the compiler will spit out an error message. Once you have fixed it, the compiler should recompile your new JavaScript file. Remember that CoffeeScript is whitespace sensitive. If you come across any errors that you don't understand, check your indentation carefully.

Adding a to-do item

Now we can add the event handling to actually add a to-do item to the list. In our `bindEvents` function, we'll select the `new-todo` input and handle its `keyup` event. We bind that to call the `create` method on our class, which we'll also go and define; this is shown in the following code snippet:

```
bindEvents: ->
  $('#new-todo').on('keyup', @create)

create: (e) ->
  $input = $(this)
  val = ($.trim $input.val())
  return unless e.which == 13 and val
  alert val
  # We create the todo item
```

The `$('#new-todo')` function uses the jQuery CSS selector syntax to get the input with the `new-todo` ID, the `on` method binds the `create` method to its `'keyup'` event, which fires whenever a key is pressed while the input has focus.

In the `create` function, we can get a reference to the input by using the `$(this)` function, which will always return the element that generated the event. We assign this to the `$input` variable. Using variable names that are prefixed with `$` is a common convention when assigning jQuery variables. We can then get the value of the input using the `val()` function and assign it a local `val` variable.

We can see if the *Enter* key was pressed by checking if the `which` property of the `keyup` event is equal to `13`. If so, and if the `val` variable is not `null`, we can go ahead and create the to-do item. For now, we'll just output its value using an alert message.

Once we create the item, where shall we put it? In lots of traditional web apps, this data will typically be stored on the server using an Ajax request. We would like to keep this app simple for now and just keep these items around on the client side for now. The HTML5 specification defines a mechanism for us called **localStorage**, to do just that.

Using localStorage

`localStorage` is part of the new HTML5 specification and allows you to store and retrieve objects in a local database that lives in the browser. The interface is quite simple; in supported browsers a global variable named `localStorage` will be present. This variable has the following three important methods:

```
localStorage.setItem(key, value)
localStorage.getItem(key)
localStorage.removeItem(key)
```

Both the `key` and `value` parameters are strings. Strings stored in the `localStorage` variable hang around even when the page is refreshed. You can store up to 5 MB in the `localStorage` variable in most browsers.

Because we want to store the to-do items as a complex object rather than a string, we use the commonly used technique of converting to and from a JSON object when setting and getting items from `localStorage`. To do so, we'll add two methods to the prototype of the `Storage` class, which will then be available on the global `localStorage` object. Add the following code snippet to the top of our `app.coffee` file:

```
Storage::setObj = (key, obj) ->
  @setItem key, JSON.stringify(obj)

Storage::getObj = (key) ->
  JSON.parse @getItem(key)
```

Here, we use the `::` operator to add the `setObj` and `getObj` methods to the `Storage` class. These functions wrap the `localStorage` object's `getItem` and `setItem` methods by converting the object to and from JSON.

We are now finally ready to create our to-do item and store it in `localStorage`.

Here is the rest of our `create` method:

```
create: (e)->
  $input = $(this)
  val = ($.trim $input.val())
  return unless e.which == 13 and val

  randomId = (Math.floor Math.random()*999999)

  localStorage.setObj randomId,{
    id: randomId
    title: val
    completed: false
  }
  $input.val ''
```

In order for us to uniquely identify tasks, we'll use the simplest thing we can, and just generate a big random number to use as an ID. This is not the most sophisticated way of identifying documents and you should probably not use this in a production setting. However, it's quite simple to implement, and serves our purposes well for now.

After generating the ID, we can now put the to-do item in our local database using our `setObj` method. We pass in a title that we got from the `input` tag value, and default the item to not completed.

Lastly, we clear the value of `$input` to give the user visual input that `create` was successful.

We should now be able to test our little app and see if the to-do items do get stored into `localStorage`. The Google Chrome Developer Tools will allow you to inspect `localStorage` in the **Resources** tab. After adding a couple of tasks, you should be able to see them here, as shown in the following screenshot:

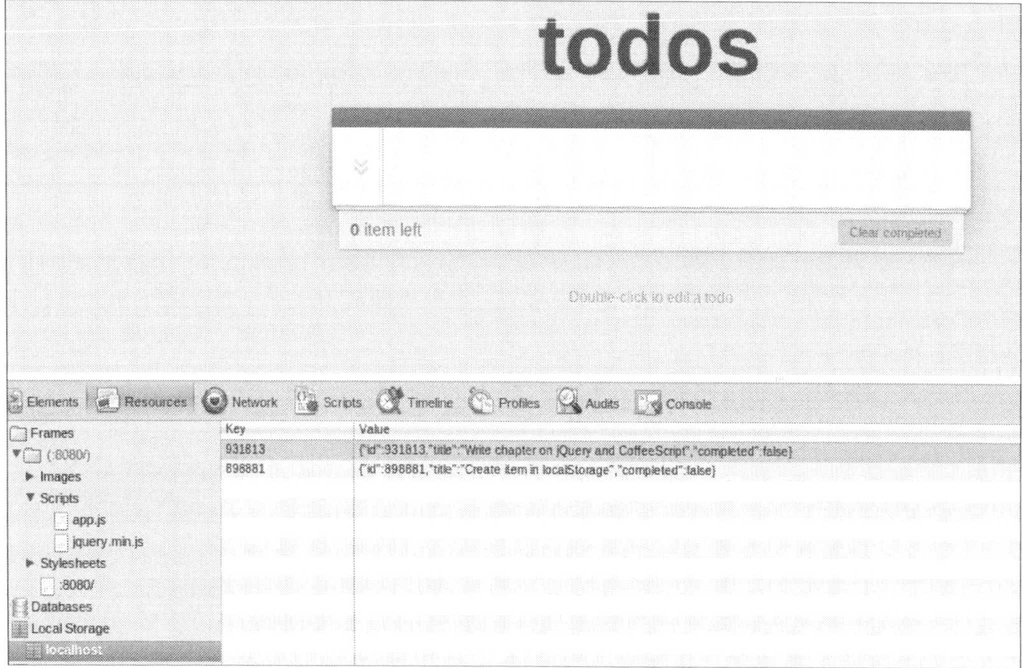

Displaying the to-do items

Now that we can store a list of to-do items, it would be nice if we could see them on screen. To do so, we will add a `displayItems` method. This will iterate through the local list of to-do items and display them.

Add the following code to our `TodoApp`, after the `create` method:

```
displayItems: ->
    alert 'displaying items'
```

Now we should be able to call this method from the `create` method, as highlighted in the following code:

```
create: (e) ->
  $input = $(this)
  val = ($.trim $input.val())
  return unless e.which == 13 and val

  randomId = (Math.floor Math.random()*999999)

  localStorage.setObj randomId,{
    id: randomId
    title: val
    completed: false
  }
  $input.val ''
  @displayItems()
```

Let's run this code to see what happens. When we do, we get the following error:

Uncaught TypeError: Object #<HTMLInputElement> has no method 'displayItems'

So what's happening here? It seems that the call to `@displayItems()` is trying to call the method on an instance of `HTMLInputElement` instead of `TodoApp`.

This happens because jQuery will set the value of `this` to reference the element that raised the event. When we bind a class method as an event handler, jQuery will in essence "highjack" `this` to not point to the class itself. It is an important caveat that you should know of when working with jQuery and classes in CoffeeScript.

To fix it, we can use the CoffeeScript fat arrow when we set up the `keyup` event handler, which will ensure that the value of `this` remains intact. Let's modify our `bindEvents` method to look similar to the following code:

```
bindEvents: ->
  $('#new-todo').on('keyup',(e) => @create(e))
```

There is just one more thing though; in our `createItem` method, we used `$(this)` to get the value of the `input` element that raised the event. Since switching to the fat arrow, this will now be pointing to our `TodoApp` instance. Luckily, the event argument that gets passed in has a target property that also points to our input. Change the first line of the `create` method similar to the following code snippet:

```
create: (e) ->
  $input = $(e.target)
  val = ($.trim $input.val())
```

Now when we create an item, we should see the "displaying items" alert, meaning the `displayItems` method has been hooked up correctly.

We can do one better. Since the `$input` tag will need to be looked up every time the `create` method is fired, we can just store it in a class variable so that it can be re-used.

The best place for this would be right when the app starts up. Let's create a `cacheElements` method that does just that, and gets called in the constructor—this is highlighted in the following code:

```
class TodoApp

  constructor: ->
    @cacheElements()
    @bindEvents()

  cacheElements: ->
    @$input = $('#new-todo')

  bindEvents: ->
    @$input.on('keyup',(e) => @create(e))

  create: (e) ->
    val = ($.trim @$input.val())
    return unless e.which == 13 and val

    randomId = (Math.floor Math.random()*999999)

    localStorage.setObj randomId,{
      id: randomId
      title: val
        completed: false
    }
    @$input.val ''
  @displayItems()
```

The `cacheElements` call assigns a class variable called `@$input`, which is then used throughout our class. This `@$` syntax might look strange at first, but it does convey a lot of information in a few keystrokes.

Showing the to-do items

We should now be able to show the items. In the `displayItems` method, we'll iterate through all the `localStorage` keys and use them to get each corresponding to-do item. For each item we'll add a `li` child element to the `ul` element with the `todo-list` ID. Before we start working with the `$('#todo-list')` element, let's cache its value like we did with `@$input`:

```
  cacheElements: ->
    @$input = $('#new-todo')
    @$todoList = $('#todo-list')
  displayItems: ->
    @clearItems()
    @addItem(localStorage.getObj(id)) for id in Object.
keys(localStorage)

  clearItems: ->
    @$todoList.empty()

  addItem: (item) ->
    html = """
      <li #{if item.completed then 'class="completed"' else ''} data-
id="#{item.id}">
        <div class="view">
          <input class="toggle" type="checkbox" #{if item.completed
then 'checked' else ''}>
          <label>#{item.title}</label>
          <button class="destroy"></button>
        </div>
     </li>
    """
    @$todoList.append(html)
```

Here, we have modified the `displayItems` method a bit. First, we remove any existing child list items from `$@todoList`, then we loop through each key in `localStorage`, get the object with that key, and send that item to the `addItem` method.

The `addItem` method builds an HTML string representation of a to-do item and then uses jQuery's `append` function to append a child element to `$@todoList`. Together with a label for the title, we also create a checkbox to set the task as completed and a button to remove the task.

Notice the `data-id` attribute on the `li` element. This is an HTML5 data attribute, which lets you add arbitrary data attributes to any element. We will use this to link each `li` to its to-do item in the `localStorage` object.

> Although CoffeeScript can make building HTML strings like these a bit easier, it can quickly become cumbersome to define markup within your client-side code. We have done so here mostly for illustration purposes; it's probably better to use a JavaScript templating library, such as Handlebars (`http://handlebarsjs.com/`).
>
> These types of libraries allow you define templates within your markup and then compile them with a specific context, which then gives you a nicely formatted HTML that you can then append to the elements.

One last thing, now that we can display items after one is created, let's add the `displayItems` call to the constructor, so that we can display existing to-do items; this call is highlighted in the following code:

```
constructor: ->
  @cacheElements()
  @bindEvents()
  @displayItems()
```

Removing and completing items

Let's hook up the remove task button. We add an event handler for it follows:

```
bindEvents: ->
  @$input.on('keyup',(e) => @create(e))
  @$todoList.on('click', '.destroy', (e) => @destroy(e.target))
```

Here, we handle click events on any child element on `@$todoList` with a `.destroy` class.

We once again create the handler with the fat arrow, calling a `@destroy` method and passing in the target, which should be the **destroy** button that was clicked.

We now need to create the `@destroy` method using the following code snippet:

```
destroy: (elem) ->
  id = $(elem).closest('li').data('id')
  localStorage.removeItem(id)
  @displayItems()
```

The `closest` function will find the `li` element that is defined nearest to the button itself. We use jQuery's `data` function to retrieve its `data-id` attribute, which we can then use to remove the to-do item from `localStorage`. One more call is made to `@displayItems` to refresh the view.

Completing an item will follow a very similar pattern; that is, we add an event handler, which is highlighted in the following code:

```
bindEvents: ->
  @$input.on('keyup',(e) => @create(e))
  @$todoList.on('click', '.destroy', (e) => @destroy(e.target))
  @$todoList.on('change', '.toggle', (e) => @toggle(e.target))
```

This time we handle the `'change'` event, which will fire whenever a completed checkbox is checked or unchecked. This in turn will call the `@toggle` method, which is coded as follows:

```
toggle: (elem) ->
  id = $(elem).closest('li').data('id')
  item = localStorage.getObj(id)
  item.completed = !item.completed
  localStorage.setObj(id, item)
```

This method also uses the `closest` function to get the ID of the to-do item. It loads up the object from `localStorage`, toggles the value of `completed`, and then saves it back to `localStorage` using the `setObj` method.

Now, it's your turn!

As a final exercise for you, I will ask you to make the **Clear completed** button work.

Summary

In this chapter, we learned what jQuery is, and what its strengths and benefits are. We also learned how to combine the powerful features of jQuery with CoffeeScript to write complex web applications with much less effort and complexity. jQuery is a very large library and we have just scratched the surface of what it has to offer. I urge you to spend some more time learning the library itself, and to do so using CoffeeScript.

Next up, we'll start by having a look at how you would start interacting with sever-side code using CoffeeScript and Rails.

4
CoffeeScript and Rails

Ruby on Rails is a web framework that came around in 2004. It was written by David Heinemeier Hansson and was extracted as a framework from **Basecamp**, a project management web application he had written in Ruby for his company **37signals**.

Rails immediately impressed a lot of people by how effortlessly and quickly one could go about writing web applications and soon became quite popular.

At the time it was developed, Ruby was an obscure scripting language from Japan that no one had really heard of. Ruby was really at the heart of why Rails was so successful. It has proved to be a powerful and succinct programming language, and many programmers have stated that it makes programming fun again.

What makes Rails special?

Rails has pushed the envelope on how web developers approach writing applications. Its core philosophy consists of the following two important principles:

- Convention over configuration
- Don't repeat yourself, or DRY

Convention over configuration

Rails is designed to assume that the programmer will follow certain known conventions, which if used, provide great benefit and much less need to configure the framework. It's often called an opinionated framework. That means that the framework makes assumptions on how a typical application should be built and structured and it doesn't try to be overly flexible and configurable. This helps you spend less time on mundane tasks like configuring and wiring up an application architecture and more time on actually building your app.

For instance, Rails will model tables in your database with objects corresponding to their names, so a record in the `Transactions` database will automatically map to a `Transactions` class instance, as will a record in the `people` database table automatically map to a `Person` class instance.

Rails will generally use conventions to do smart things for you. Let's say our `people` table also has a `datetime` field called `created_at` and `updated_at`. Rails will be smart enough to now automatically update the timestamps on these two fields when a record gets created or updated.

The most important thing about Rails' conventions is that you should know about them and not fight the framework, or try to diverge too much from the Rails way, without good reason. Often, this can cancel out any of the benefits you get from these conventions, or even make it harder on yourself to try and find workarounds.

Don't repeat yourself (DRY)

This software engineering principle can also be stated as follows:

> *Every piece of knowledge must have a single, unambiguous, and authoritative representation within a system.*

This means that Rails strives to remove duplication and boilerplate wherever it can.

For instance, a `Person` class that models records in the `people` table will not need to define its fields, since they are already defined as columns in your database table. Here, Rails can use the powerful metaprogramming capabilities of Ruby to magically add attributes to the `Person` class that correspond to columns in your database.

> **Metaprogramming** is the concept of writing code that acts on other code as data structures. In other words, metaprogramming is writing code that writes code. It is used heavily in the Ruby community and the Rails source code in particular.
>
> The Ruby language has very powerful metaprogramming abilities that are tied to the concept of open classes and objects, meaning that you can easily "open up" an existing class definition and redefine and add members to it.

Rails and JavaScript

For a long time, Rails was shipped with the `Prototype.js` and `Script.aculo.us` JavaScript libraries for AJAX, page animation, and effects.

Rails has the concept of view helpers—these are Ruby methods that can be used in views to abstract away common HTML constructs. Many of the view helpers that deal with client-side code and AJAX were built on top of these two frameworks, and thus they were completely baked in the framework without an easy way of using alternatives.

`Prototype.js` shares many of the same ideas and goals as jQuery, but over time, jQuery has grown to be perceived as a more elegant and powerful library by many programmers.

As jQuery became more popular, many developers in the Rails community started experimenting by using jQuery with Rails instead of the default JavaScript libraries. A standard set of libraries or **gems** emerged for replacing the built-in Prototype library with jQuery.

In Rails Version 3.1, it was announced that jQuery will be the default JavaScript library. Because jQuery already had most of the animation and page effect features of `Script.aculo.us`, this library was also not needed anymore.

This move seemed to have been a long time coming and generally had the blessings of most of the Rails community.

Rails and CoffeeScript

Another big addition to Rails 3.1 was the asset pipeline. Its main goal is to make it easy to treat assets such as JavaScript and CSS as first-class citizens in your Rails app. Prior to this, JavaScript and CSS were just served as static content. It also provides an organizational skeleton that helps you to organize your JavaScript and CSS and provides a DSL for accessing them.

With the asset pipeline, you can organize and manage dependencies between assets using manifest files. Rails will also use the pipeline to minify and concatenate JavaScript as well as apply fingerprints for cache busting.

The asset pipeline also has a pre-processor chain that will allow you to run files through a series of input-output processors before they are served. It knows which pre-processors to run using file extension names.

Before Rails 3.1 was released, it was announced that the CoffeeScript compiler would be supported out of the box using the asset pipeline. This was a huge announcement since CoffeeScript is still quite a young language and it stoked quite some controversy within the Rails community, with some lamenting the fact that they didn't want to learn or use this new language.

The Rails maintainers have stuck to their guns though, and at present it couldn't be easier to use CoffeeScript in Rails. The fact that CoffeeScript is the default for writing client-side JavaScript code has been a huge boost for CoffeeScript, and a lot of Rails developers have since gotten to know and embraced the language.

We've been going on about how wonderful Rails is and how well it works with CoffeeScript, so let's get Rails installed so that you can see for yourself what all the fuss is about.

Installing Rails

There are many different ways of installing Ruby and Rails on your development machine depending on your operating system, which version of Ruby you would like to use, if you're using version managers, building from source, and dozens of other options. In this book, we will only briefly cover the most common ways of installing it on Windows, Mac, and Linux. Please note that in this book we'll be using a Rails version of at least 3.2 and higher and Ruby 1.9.2 and higher.

Installing Rails using RailsInstaller

On Windows, or optionally on a Mac, I would recommend **RailsInstaller** (`http://railsinstaller.org/`). It contains everything you need to start with Rails, including the latest version of Ruby itself. After downloading the setup program, installation couldn't be much easier; just run it and step through the wizard. After the installation, you should be presented with an open console command prompt. Try entering `rails -v`. If you see a version number, you should be good to go.

Installing Rails using RVM

Installing Ruby and Rails on a Mac and Linux can be really easy using **RVM**, or the **Ruby Version Manager**, from `https://rvm.io/`.

The Ruby language has grown to be very popular over the past few years, and this has resulted in multiple implementations of the language being written, which can run on difference platforms. **Matz's Ruby Interpreter** (**MRI**), the standard implementation of Ruby, has also gone through several versions. RVM is great for managing and installing different versions of Ruby. It comes with a one-stop installer bash script that will install both the latest Ruby and Rails. Just run the following command from the terminal:

```
curl -L https://get.rvm.io | bash -s stable --rails
```

This might take quite a while to finish. Once it's done, you should try entering `rails -v` in the terminal. If you see a version number of at least 3.2, you should be good to go.

Got Rails installed?

Now that we have Rails installed, let's go ahead and build an application using CoffeeScript.

If you ran into any problem or want more information on installing Rails, the best place to start would be on the **Download** section of the Ruby on Rails site (`http://rubyonrails.org/download`).

Developing our Rails application

We'll take parts of our existing to-do list application and extend it with a server-side backend using Rails. If you weren't following along in the previous chapter, then you should be able to just copy the code for that chapter as needed.

> This chapter isn't meant to be a complete introduction to all of Ruby on Rails or Ruby, the language. Here, we would like to focus on building a simple Rails app within the context of how you would go about using Rails with CoffeeScript.
>
> We will not go into everything in too much detail, and we'll trust in the fact that Ruby is quite a simple and readable language and that Rails code is simple to understand. Even if you aren't familiar with the language and the framework, it should not be too hard to follow along.

First, we'll start out by creating an empty base Rails application using the `rails` command. Navigate to a folder where you would like to create your app and then run this command:

```
rails new todo
```

This will create a `todo` folder with a whole bunch of files and folders for your web application. In Rails' spirit of following conventions, your web application will be organized in a certain manner.

> The `rails` command is used for many things besides generating a new application and serves as your entry point into many of the common day-to-day Rails tasks. We'll be covering a few of them in this book and if you want to see the full list of what it can do, you can run `rails -h`.

Let's briefly talk about how Rails organizes our application. Most of your application code will probably live in the top-level `app` folder. This folder contains the following four important subfolders:

- `assets`: This is the folder from which the asset pipeline operates. This is where all your CoffeeScript (or JavaScript) and CSS source code, as well as images used by our web app, will be.
- `controllers`: This is where your controllers live. These are responsible for handling routed requests for the application and they talk to your views and models.
- `models`: This is where you'll find the domain models. Models represent domain objects in a system and correspond to database tables using the `ActiveRecord` base class.
- `views`: This folder contains view templates that are used to render your application's HTML. By default, Rails uses ERB templates, which allow us to include snippets of Ruby code within an HTML template that will be evaluated to generate the final output HTML.

MVC

MVC, or **Model-View-Controller**, is a widely used application architecture pattern that aims to simplify code and reduce coupling by splitting application concerns into three domain object types.

Rails follows the MVC pattern very closely, and most Rails applications will be structured very heavily in terms of models, controllers, and views.

Another pattern on top of MVC that has been espoused by many Rails programmers over the last few years is fat models, skinny controllers. This concept encourages the practice of placing most of your domain logic within models, and that controllers should only be concerned about routing and interaction between models and views.

Running our application

At this stage we can already run our Rails application to see if it all worked. From the terminal, enter:

```
cd todo
rails server
```

Rails will now start hosting a local web server for our application on port **3000**. You can test it by browsing to `http://localhost:3000/`. If all went well, then you should see the following friendly welcome message:

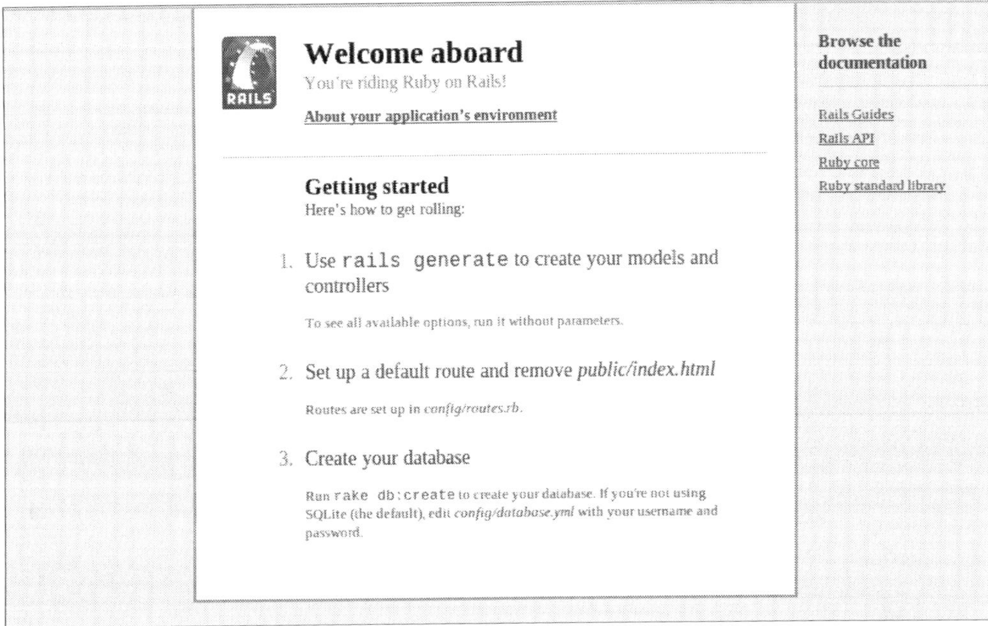

Remember to keep this server running in a separate console window as we test our application. You can also check the output of this process for any errors that might occur while it's running.

Our todo_items resource

So, we now have a running application, but it doesn't do much except show us a welcome page.

To get to our goal of being able to track to-do tasks, we'll generate a resource for our to-do items. In Rails parlance, a resource consists of a model, a controller with some actions, as well as views for those actions.

At the terminal, run the following command:

```
rails generate resource todo_item title:string completed:boolean
```

What did this do? This is an example of Rails' generator syntax, which can be used to generate boilerplate code. Here, we tell it to create a "resourceful" controller named `TodoItemsController` and a model, `TodoItem`, which has a `string` field for its title and a `boolean` flag to mark it as completed.

As you can see from the command output, it has generated a bunch of files as well as modified an existing one, in `config/routes.rb`. Let's start by opening this file.

routes.rb

Here is what you should see at the top of the `routes.rb` file:

```
Todo::Application.routes.draw do
  resources :todo_items
```

In Rails, `routes.rb` defines how HTTP calls to URLs map to controller actions that can handle them.

Here, the generator added a line for us, which uses the `resources` method. This method creates the routes for the most common actions of a "resourceful" controller. This means it exposes a single domain resource in your application using the HTTP verbs, GET, POST, PUT, and DELETE.

Usually, this will create routes for seven different controller actions, `index`, `show`, `new`, `create`, `edit`, `update`, and `destroy`. As you will see later on, we won't need to create all these actions for our controller, so we'll tell the `resources` method to filter out only the ones we want. Modify the file to look like the following code snippet:

```
Todo::Application.routes.draw do
  resources :todo_items, only: [:index, :create, :update, :destroy]
```

The controller

In the call to `resources`, Rails uses the `:todo_items` symbol to conventionally map the `resources` method to `TodoItemsController`, which was also generated for us.

Open the `app/controllers/todo_items_controller.rb` file; here is what you'll see:

```
class TodoItemsController < ApplicationController
end
```

As you can see, there isn't a whole lot in here. A class named `TodoItemController` is declared, and it derives from the `ApplicationController` class. The `ApplicationController` class was also generated for us when we created the app, and it derives from `ActionController::Base`, which gives it a whole lot of functionality and lets it behave like a Rails controller.

We should now be able to test out our controller by navigating to the `http://localhost:3000/todo_items` URL.

What do you see? You should get the **Unknown action** error page stating that the `index` action could not be found for `TodoItemsController`.

This is because the controller doesn't yet have an `index` action defined, as specified in our `routes.rb` file. Let's go ahead and add a method to our `TodoItemsController` class to handle that action; this is shown in the following code snippet:

```
class TodoItemsController < ApplicationController
  def index
  end
end
```

If we refresh the page, we get a different error message: **Template is missing**. This happens because we don't have a template for the `index` action. By default, Rails will always try to return a rendered template that corresponds to the `index` action name. Let's go ahead and add one now.

The view

Rails views are saved in the `app/views` folder. Each controller will have a subfolder here containing its views. We already have an `index.html` file from the previous chapter, which we'll re-use here. To do this, we'll need to copy everything that is inside the `body` tag, excluding the last two `script` tags from the old `index.html` file, into a file called `app/views/todo_items/index.html.erb`.

You should end up with the following markup:

```
<section id="todoapp">
  <header id="header">
    <h1>todos</h1>
    <input id="new-todo" placeholder="What needs to be done?"
autofocus>
  </header>
  <section id="main">
    <ul id="todo-list">

    </ul>
  </section>
  <footer id="footer">
      <button id="clear-completed">Clear completed</button>
  </footer>
</section>
```

Looking at this, you might be wondering where the rest of the HTML such as the enclosing `html`, `head`, and `body` tags have gone.

Well, Rails has the concept of a layout file, which acts as a wrapper for all the other views. This way you can have a consistent skeleton for your site that you don't need to create for each view. Our view will be embedded inside the default layout file: `app/views/layouts/application.html.erb`. Let's have a look at that file:

```
<!DOCTYPE html>
<html>
<head>
  <title>Todo</title>
  <%= stylesheet_link_tag    "application", :media => "all" %>
  <%= javascript_include_tag "application" %>
  <%= csrf_meta_tags %>
</head>
<body>

<%= yield %>

</body>
</html>
```

The `stylesheet_link_tag` and `javascript_include_tag` methods will make sure that all the files specified in the `assets` folder are included in the HTML. The `<%= yield %>` line is where the current view will be rendered, which is `index.html.erb` in our case.

When we refresh the page now, we'll see the `index` page. Have a look at the source code to get an idea of how the final HTML is output.

As you can see, our page is still unstyled and looks quite dull. Let's see if we can make it look pretty again.

The CSS

By default, the asset pipeline will look for CSS files in the `app/assets/stylesheets` folder. When we browse to this folder, we'll see a file named `todo_items.css.scss`, which was generated for us when we created the controller.

Copy the contents of the previous chapter's `styles.css` file into this file. Our `index` page should now look decent again.

This file with the strange `.css.scss` extension is a Saas file (`http://sass-lang.com/`).

Like CoffeeScript, Sass is an extended version of the normal CSS language, with a lot of nice features that make writing CSS easier and less repetitive.

As with CoffeeScript, it is the default CSS compiler in the Rails asset pipeline. The flavor of Sass that we're using is a superset of CSS, which means we can use normal CSS in this file without using any of the Sass features and it will work fine.

Our model

So now we can see our to-do list, but we don't have any items showing up. This time, instead of storing them locally, we'll store them in the database. Luckily for us, we already have a database model that was generated for us when we created the resource and the `TodoItem` model, which is defined in `app/models/todo_item.rb`:

```
class TodoItem < ActiveRecord::Base
  attr_accessible :completed, :title
end
```

Here, like with controllers, you can see that Rails models get most of their functionality by deriving from `ActiveRecord::Base`. The `attr_accessible` line tells `ActiveRecord` which fields on this model can be assigned to and from user input.

How do we use the model? Add the following highlighted code in `todo_items_controller.rb`:

```
def index
  @todo_items = TodoItem.all
end
```

This line uses an `all` class method on the `TodoItem` class, which is also provided by `ActiveRecord`. This will return a new instance of the `TodoItem` class for each record in the database, which we can assign to an instance variable called `@todo_items` (in Ruby all instance variables start with an `@` symbol).

When Rails executes a controller action, it will automatically make any of the controller instance variables available to the view being rendered, which is why we're assigning it here. We'll get to use it in our view soon.

Let's refresh the page again to see if this worked. Yet again, we get a **Could not find table 'todo_items'** error.

You've probably guessed that we're supposed to create a table called `todo_items` in a database somewhere. Luckily, Rails has already taken care of the hard work, using something called migration.

Migrations

When we generated our resource, Rails not only created a model for us, but also a database script written in Ruby, or **migration**. We should be able to open it in the `db/migrations` folder. The actual file will be prefixed with a timestamp and will end with `_create_todo_items.rb`. It should look similar to the following code snippet:

```
class CreateTodoItems < ActiveRecord::Migration
  def change
    create_table :todo_items do |t|
      t.string :title
      t.boolean :completed

      t.timestamps
    end
  end
end
```

This script will create a table named `todo_items` with the fields that we had specified when we generated the `todo_item` resource. It also creates two timestamp fields named `created_at` and `updated_at` using the `t.timestamps` method. Rails will make sure that fields with those names get updated with the appropriate timestamp when a record gets created or updated.

Migration scripts are a wonderful way of automating database changes, even allowing you to roll back a previous change. You don't have to rely on migrations created by resource or model generators either. Custom migrations can be generated by running the following command:

```
rails generate migration migration_name
```

After generating your custom migration, you can just implement the `up` and `down` methods, which will be called when your migration gets executed or rolled back.

Migrations are executed with the `rake` command. `rake` is a task-management tool that allows you to write tasks as Ruby scripts, which are then run using the `rake` command-line utility. Rails comes with a whole lot of built-in `rake` tasks, and you can see the full list of them by using:

```
rake -T
```

The task that we're interested in the moment is called `db:migrate`, let's run it and see what happens:

```
rake db:migrate
```

You should see the following output:

== CreateTodoItems: migrating ==
===========

-- create_table(:todo_items)

-> 0.0011s

== CreateTodoItems: migrated (0.0013s) ==================================
========

This means Rails has successfully created a `todo_items` table for us in the database. When we refresh the application page, we should see that the error is gone and we're seeing our blank to-do list.

Where is the database?

You might have wondered where our actual database lives at the moment. Rails defaults to using an embedded SQLite database. SQLite (`http://www.sqlite.org`) is a self-contained, file-based database that doesn't need a server to be configured for it to run. This makes it really nice and easy to get up and running quickly when developing an application.

Once you actually deploy your web app, you would probably want to go with a more traditional database server, such as MySQL or PostgreSQL. You can easily change your database connection settings in the `config/database.yml` file.

We still haven't hooked up our view to actually show the list of to-do items. Before we do that, let's manually create a couple of to-do items in the database.

The Rails console

Rails has a nifty way of interactively playing with your code by using the Rails console. This is an interactive Ruby interpreter, or **irb**, session with all the Rails project code loaded. Let's fire it up by using the following command:

```
rails console
```

Once you're in the console you can enter any valid Ruby code. You can also access all the models in your Rails app. Let's try it with the `TodoItem.all` method that we used earlier; this is shown in the following screenshot:

```
michael@walrus ~/dev/todo $ rails console
Loading development environment (Rails 3.2.6)
1.9.3p125 :001 > TodoItem.all
  TodoItem Load (0.1ms)  SELECT "todo_items".* FROM "todo_items"
 => []
1.9.3p125 :002 >
```

At the moment it returns an empty array, since our table is still empty. Notice that Rails also outputted the SQL query that it has generated to get all the records.

From here we can also create a new to-do item using our model. The following code will do that:

```
TodoItem.create(title: "Hook up our index view", completed: false)
```

Now, we should have a single to-do item in our table. You can verify this by using `TodoItem.first`, which will return the first item in our table.

I want to make sure that our model always has a title. `ActiveRecord` has very powerful validation features that are built-in, which allows for specifying constraints on model attributes in a very declarative manner. Let's make sure that our model always checks for the presence of a title before saving; to do this, add the following highlighted code:

```
class TodoItem < ActiveRecord::Base
  attr_accessible :completed, :title
  validates :title,  :presence => true
end
```

Go ahead and create a couple of other to-do items. Once you have done this, try running `TodoItem.all` again. This time it returns an array of `TodoItem` instances.

To exit the rails console, just enter `exit`.

Displaying the items in our view using ERB

To display our to-do items in our view, we'll use the `@todo_items` instance variable that we created in our controller action. Let's modify the `app/views/todo_items.html.erb` file and mix in some Ruby using ERB; add the code that is highlighted in the following code snippet:

```
<section id="todoapp">
  <header id="header">
    <h1>todos</h1>
    <input id="new-todo" placeholder="What needs to be done?"
autofocus>
  </header>
  <section id="main">
    <ul id="todo-list">
      <% @todo_items.each do |item| %>
        <li class="<%= item.completed ? "completed" : "" %>" data-
id="<%= item.id %>">
          <div class="view">
            <input class="toggle" type="checkbox" <%= "checked" if
item.completed %>>
            <label><%= item.title %></label>
            <button class="destroy"></button>
          </div>
        </li>
      <% end %>
    </ul>
  </section>
  <footer id="footer">
      <button id="clear-completed">Clear completed</button>
  </footer>
</section>
```

ERB templates are quite simple to understand. The basic idea is that you write your HTML as normal and mix in Ruby using ERB tags. The following three tags are important:

```
<% These tags will be just be executed  %>
<%= These should contain a Ruby expression that will be evaluated and
included in the document %>
<%# This is a comment and will be ignored %>
```

In our `index` ERB template, we use Ruby's `each` iterator to loop through all the elements in the `@todo_items` array instance variable; `each` takes a Ruby block as an argument. A block is a piece of code that can be passed to a method as data, similar to how functions can be passed as arguments in CoffeeScript.

This block will be executed for each item in the array, passing it in as the item variable. For each item, we create its markup, using the item's `title` and `completed` attributes inside of our ERB tags.

When we refresh the page, we should now finally see our list of to-do items! If you are curious, have a look at the HTML source of the document and compare it to the ERB template, this should give you a good idea of how it was generated. The output page is shown in the following screenshot:

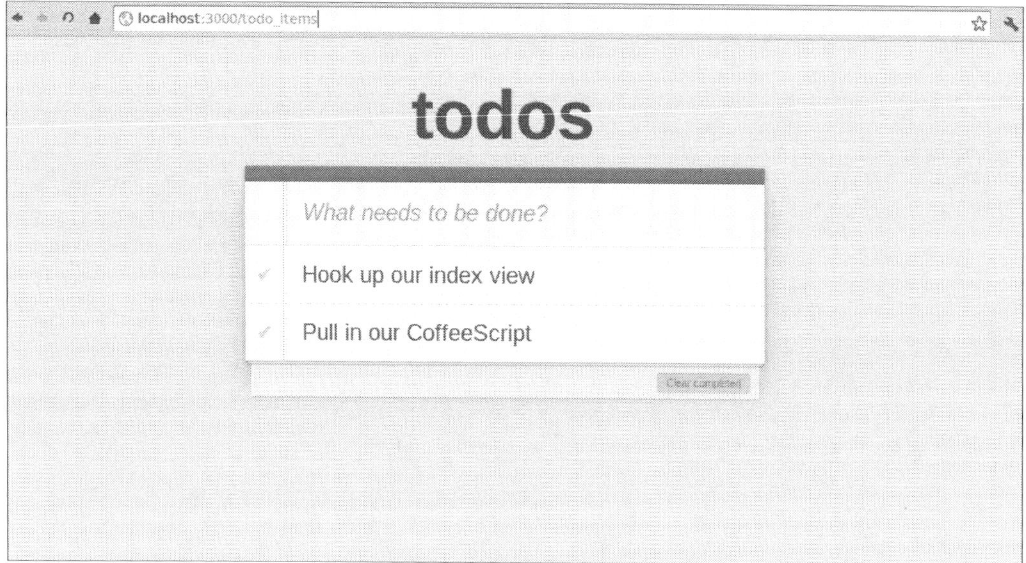

Creating a partial

At the moment, our view code is starting to get a bit messy, especially the to-do items list. We can clean it up a bit by using a **view partial**, which allows us to pull out snippets of our view into a separate file. This can then be rendered where we need it in the main view. Add the line of code highlighted in the following code snippet to your file:

```
<section id="main">
  <ul id="todo-list">
    <% @todo_items.each do |item| %>
      <%= render partial: 'todo_item', locals: {item: item} %>
    <% end %>
  </ul>

</section>
```

We'll move the to-do item markup to its own partial file. By convention, partial filenames start with an underscore, and when rendering a partial, Rails will look for a file with the same name as the specified partial, with a leading underscore. Go ahead and create a file: `app/views/todo_items/_todo_item.html.erb` with the following content:

```
<li class="<%= item.completed ? "completed" : "" %>" data-id="<%=
item.id %>">
  <div class="view">
    <input class="toggle" type="checkbox" <%= "checked" if item.
completed %>>
    <label><%= item.title %></label>
    <button class="destroy"></button>
  </div>
</li>
```

If all went well, our view should still work as before, and we have cleaned up the main view code nicely. Simplifying views with partials are also great for reusability, which we'll see later on.

Our to-do list app still needs some work. At the moment, we can't add new tasks and the completed task and delete actions don't work either. This calls for some client-side code, which means we can finally start using some CoffeeScript.

Adding new items

To add new items to our to-do list, we'll use some of Rails' native AJAX capabilities. The following code snippet is a modified version of the `todo` i nput on our `index` view:

```
  <header id="header">
    <h1>todos</h1>
    <%= form_for TodoItem.new, :method => :post, :remote => true do
|f| %>
      <%= f.text_field :title, id:'new-todo', placeholder: 'What needs
to be done?', autofocus: true  %>
    <% end %>
  </header>
```

So what has changed here? First, you'll notice that we have included the `form_for` method, with another call to `text_field` inside of its block. These are Rails' view helpers, which are Ruby methods available inside of views, that provide ways of building the HTML output.

The `form_for` method will output an HTML `form` tag, and the `text_field` method will generate an `input` tag inside the form, which will be of type `text`.

We pass a new instance of `TodoItem` as a parameter to the `form_for` method. Rails is smart enough to know from the `TodoItem` instance that the form's URL should point to `TodoItemController`, and will use attributes of the `TodoItem` model as names of inputs inside the form.

The real magic comes in with the `:remote => true` parameter sent to the `form_for` method. This tells Rails that you want this form to be submitted using AJAX. Rails will take care of all of this in the background.

So which controller action will my form be submitted to? Since we specified its action as `post`, it will map to a `create` action in `TodoItemController`. We don't have one yet, so let's go and write it:

```
def create
  @todo_item = TodoItem.create(params[:todo_item])
end
```

Here, we create `TodoItem` using the `:todo_item` key in `params`—`params`, which is a Ruby hash that Rails created. It contains a value with the key, `:todo_items`, which is a hash containing all the parameter values that were submitted from the form. When we pass this hash to the `TodoItem.create` method, Rails will know how to map them to attributes on our new model and save it to the database.

Let's try and add a to-do item

Type a title in our input box for a new to-do item and hit *Enter*.

However, it seems like nothing happened. We can head over to the output of our running Rails server session to see if we can spot any errors. If you scroll around a bit, you should see an error similar to the following error message:

ActionView::MissingTemplate (Missing template todo_items/create, application/create with {:locale=>[:en], :formats=>[:js, "application/

ecmascript", "application/x-ecmascript", :html, :text, :js, :css, :ics, :csv, :png, :jpeg, :gif, :bmp, :tiff, :mpeg, :xml, :rss, :atom,

:yaml, :multipart_form, :url_encoded_form, :json, :pdf, :zip], :handlers=>[:erb, :builder, :coffee]}. Searched in:

*** "/home/michael/dev/todo/app/views"**

)

Adding a CoffeeScript view

So, it seems we still need to do one more thing. All controller actions will try and render a view by default. When we try adding a to-do item now, we would get the same **Template is missing** error as earlier. It might not be clear what should happen, since the form was posted using AJAX. Should we still render a view? And how would it look?

Looking at the error message a bit more closely might give us a clue. Since our action was invoked using AJAX, Rails will, by default, look for a CoffeeScript view to render as JavaScript.

The generated JavaScript will serve as the response to the AJAX call and will be executed on completion. This also seems like the perfect place to update our to-do items list, after creating it on the server.

We'll create a CoffeeScript view template for our `create` action in `app/views/todo_items/create.js.coffee`.

```
$('#new-todo').val('')
html = "<%= escape_javascript(render partial: 'todo_item', locals:
{item: @todo_item}) %>"
$("#todo-list").append(html)
```

Here, in the previous code snippet, we grab the `#new-todo` input and clear its value. We then render the same `todo_item` partial that we used before, passing in the `@todo_item` instance variable that we created in our controller action.

We wrap the render call in an `escape_javascript` helper method, which will ensure that any special JavaScript character will be escaped in our string. We then append the newly rendered partial to our `#todo-list` element.

Try it out. We can now finally create to-do list items!

Where did jQuery come from?

Rails already included jQuery for us. The Rails asset pipeline uses a manifest file, `app/assets/javascript/application.js` to include required dependencies, for instance jQuery.

CoffeeScript in the asset pipeline

Notice how seamless this all was? Rails treats CoffeeScript as a first-class citizen in its stack, and will make sure that the `.coffee` files get compiled into JavaScript before they are used. The fact that you can also pre-process your CoffeeScript using ERB templates on the server makes this even more powerful.

Completing the to-do items

Let's hook up this functionality. This time, we will do things a bit differently to show you a different style of writing CoffeeScript in Rails. We'll follow the more traditional approach of handling the AJAX call ourselves.

Rails has already created a file where we can put our client-side code, back when we created the controller. Each controller will get its own CoffeeScript file, which will be included in the page automatically for any action on that controller.

There is also an `application.js.coffee` file, where global client-side code can be added.

The file that we're interested in will be `app/assets/views/javascripts/todo_items.js.coffee`. We can replace the contents of it with the following code, which will handle the AJAX call when completing a task:

```
toggleItem = (elem) ->
  $li = $(elem).closest('li').toggleClass("completed")
  id = $li.data 'id'

  data = "todo_item[completed]=#{elem.checked}"
  url = "/todo_items/#{id}"
  $.ajax
    type: 'PUT'
    url: url
    data: data

$ ->
  $("#todo-list").on 'change', '.toggle', (e) -> toggleItem e.target
```

First, we define a function called `toggleItem`, which we set up to be called when a checkbox value changes. In this function we toggle the parent `li` element's `completed` class and get the ID of the to-do item using its `data` attribute. We then make an AJAX call to `TodoItemController` to update the item with the current checked value of the checkbox.

Before we can run this code, we'll need to add an `update` action to our controller, which is shown in the following code snippet:

```
def update
  item = TodoItem.find params[:id]
  item.update_attributes params[:todo_item]
  render nothing: true
end
```

`params[:id]` will be the value of the ID in the URL. We use this to find the to-do item and then call the `update_attributes` method, which do just that, update our model and save it to the database. Note that we explicitly tell Rails not to render a view here by calling `render nothing: true`.

Setting tasks to completed should now work. Notice that when you refresh the page, tasks stay completed, since they were saved to the database.

Removing tasks

For removing tasks, we'll follow a very similar pattern.

In `todo_items.js.coffee`, add the following code:

```
destroyItem = (elem) ->
  $li = $(elem).closest('li')
  id = $li.data 'id'
  url = "/todo_items/#{id}"
  $.ajax
    url: url
    type: 'DELETE'
    success: -> $li.remove()

$ ->
  $("#todo-list").on 'change', '.toggle', (e) -> toggleItem e.target
  $("#todo-list").on 'click', '.destroy', (e) -> destroyItem e.target
```

In our controller, add the following code:

```
def destroy
  TodoItem.find(params[:id]).destroy
  render nothing: true
end
```

That should be all we need to remove list items. Notice that here we only remove the element once the AJAX call was successful, by handling the `success` callback.

Now, it's your turn

As a final exercise to you, I will ask you to make the **Clear completed** button work. As a hint, you should be able to use the existing `destroyItem` method functionality.

Summary

This chapter started with a whirlwind tour of Ruby on Rails. You have hopefully grown to appreciate some of the magic that Rails offers web developers and how much fun it can be developing a Rails app. We have also spent some time discovering how easy it is to use CoffeeScript in a Rails app, and the different approaches and techniques you would typically use to write client-side code.

If you haven't done so already, I encourage you to spend some more time learning Rails as well as Ruby, and immersing yourself in the wonderful communities they support.

In the next chapter, we'll explore yet another new exciting server framework that was built using JavaScript, and how CoffeeScript relates to it.

5

CoffeeScript and Node.js

Ryan Dahl created Node.js in 2009. His goal was to create a system with which one can write network server applications having high performance, using JavaScript. At that time, JavaScript was mostly run inside browsers, so a server-side framework needed some way to run JavaScript without it. Node uses Google's V8 JavaScript engine, originally written for the Chrome browser, but since it's a separate piece of software, it can run JavaScript code anywhere. Node.js lets you write JavaScript code that can be executed on the server. It can make full use of your operating system, databases, and other external network resources.

Let's talk about some of the features of Node.js.

Node is event-driven

The Node.js framework only allows non-blocking, asynchronous I/O. This means that any I/O operation that is accessing an external resource, such as the operating system, a database, or a network resource must happen asynchronously. This works by using events, or callbacks that are fired once the operation succeeds or fails.

The benefit of this is that your application becomes much more scalable, because requests don't have to wait around for slow I/O operations to finish and can instead handle more incoming requests.

Similar frameworks do exist in other languages, such as **Twisted** and **Tornado** in Python, and **EventMachine** in Ruby. A big problem with these frameworks is that all I/O libraries they use must also be non-blocking. Often, one can end up accidentally using code that blocks an I/O operation.

Node.js was built from the ground up with an event-driven philosophy and only allows non-blocking I/O, thus avoiding this problem.

Node is fast and scalable

The V8 JavaScript engine used by Node.js is highly optimized for performance, thus making Node.js applications very fast. The fact that Node is non-blocking will ensure that your applications will be able to handle many concurrent client requests without using a lot of system resources.

Node is not Rails

Although Node and Rails are often used to build similar types of applications, they are in fact, quite different. Rails strives to be a full-stack solution to building web applications, whereas Node.js is more of a low-level system for writing any type of fast and scalable network application. It does not make a lot of assumptions on how your application should be structured at all, except for the fact that you'll use an event-based architecture.

Because of this, Node developers often choose from a variety of frameworks and modules that have been built on top of Node for writing web applications, such as Express or Flatiron.

Node and CoffeeScript

As we've seen before, CoffeeScript is available as an npm module. Therefore, writing Node.js applications with CoffeeScript couldn't be much easier. In fact, the `coffee` command that we discussed earlier will run `.coffee` scripts using Node by default. To get Node installed with CoffeeScript, see *Chapter 2, Running CoffeeScript*.

"Hello World" in Node

Let's write the simplest Node app we can using CoffeeScript. Create a file named `hello.coffee` and enter the following code in it:

```
http = require('http')

server = http.createServer (req, res) ->
  res.writeHead 200
  res.end 'Hello World'

server.listen 8080
```

This uses the `http` module of Node.js, which provides capabilities for building an HTTP server. The `require('http')` function will return an instance of the `http` module, which exports a `createServer` function. This function takes a `requestListener` argument, which is a function that will respond to client requests. In this case, we respond with an HTTP status code `200` and end the response with `Hello World` as the request body. Finally, we call the `listen` method on the returned server to start it up. When this method is called, the server will listen for and handle requests until we stop it.

We can run this file with the coffee command, as shown in the following command:

```
coffee hello.coffee
```

We can test our server by browsing to `http://localhost:8080/`. We should see a simple page with only the text as **Hello World**.

Express

As you can see, Node out of the box is very low-level and bare-boned. Building web applications basically means writing a raw HTTP server. Luckily, a bunch of libraries has been developed over the last few years to help out with writing web applications on Node and to abstract away a lot of the low-level details.

Arguably, the most popular of these is **Express** (`http://expressjs.com/`). Similar to Rails, it has quite a lot of nice features that make it easier to perform common web application tasks, such as routing, rendering views, and hosting static resources.

In this chapter, we'll be writing a web application in Express using CoffeeScript.

WebSocket

Since I would like to show off some of the scalability features of Node and the types of applications that it's normally used for, we'll be making use of another interesting modern web technology, known as **WebSocket**.

The WebSocket protocol is a standard for allowing raw, bi-directional, and full-duplex (simultaneous in both directions) TCP connections over the standard HTTP port **80**. This allows for a client and server to establish a long-running TCP connection with which the server can perform push operations, which has traditionally not been possible with HTTP. It is often used in applications where there needs to be lots of low-latency interaction between the client and server.

Jade

Jade is a lightweight, markup templating language that lets you write elegant and short HTML in a syntax that closely resembles CoffeeScript. It uses quite a few features such as syntactical whitespace to reduce the number of keystrokes you need to write HTML documents. It is usually installed by default when you run Express, and we'll be using it in this book.

Our application

In this chapter, we're going to build a collaborative to-do list application. This means that you'll be able to share your to-do list with other people in real time. One or more people will be able to add, complete, or remove to-do list items at the same time. Changes to the to-do list will be automatically propagated to all users. This is the type of application that Node is perfect for.

Our Node.js code will consist of two distinct parts, the normal web application that will serve static HTML, CSS, and JavaScript, and a WebSocket server that handles the real-time updating of all the to-do list clients. Together with this, we'll have a jQuery-driven client that will look very similar to our application in *Chapter 3, CoffeeScript and jQuery*.

We'll use some of the assets (stylesheets and images) from our existing to-do list applications. We'll also re-use the client-side jQuery code from *Chapter 3, CoffeeScript and jQuery* and tweak it to fit our application. If you weren't following along in the previous chapters, you should be able to just copy assets from the code for this chapter as needed.

Let's get started

To get going, we'll do the following steps:

1. Create a folder for our application.
2. Specify our app dependencies using a `package.json` file.
3. Install our dependencies.
4. Create an `app.coffee` file.
5. Run our app for the first time.

package.json

Create a new folder named todo. Inside this folder, we'll create a file with the name package.json. Add the following code to this file:

```
{
  "name": "todo",
  "version": "0.0.1",
  "private": true,
  "scripts": {
    "start": "node app"
  },
  "dependencies": {
    "express": "3.0.0beta6",
    "jade": "*",
    "socket.io": "*",
    "coffee-script": "*",
    "connect-assets": "*"
  }
}
```

This is a simple JSON file that serves as an application manifest and is used to tell npm which dependencies you rely on in your application. Here, we're using Express as our web framework and Jade as our templating language. Since we're going to use WebSocket, we'll pull in socket.io. We can also make sure that CoffeeScript is installed by adding it to our file. Lastly, we'll use connect-assets, a module that manages client-side assets in much the same way as the Rails asset pipeline.

When dealing with the Node.js framework, you'll notice that applications are often weaved together out of npm modules in this manner. A good place to look for npm modules is the Node toolbox site (nodetoolbox.com).

Installing our modules

To install the dependencies in our package.json file, navigate to the project folder on the command-line tool and run the following command:

```
npm install
```

If all went well, then we should now have all our project dependencies installed. To verify this or just to see what npm did, you can run the following command:

```
npm ls
```

This will output a list of installed modules with their dependencies in a tree-like format.

Creating our app

All we need to run our application is to create a main, entry point file, which is used to hook up our Express application and specify our routes. In the root folder, create a file named `app.coffee`, and add the following code to it:

```
express = require 'express'
app = express()

app.get '/', (req, res) ->
  res.send('Hello Express')

app.listen(3000)
console.log('Listening on port 3000')
```

This looks very similar to our "Hello World" example.

First, we load the Express module using the `require` function. Node modules are simple; each module corresponds to a single file. Each module can declare code, which will be exported when it is required. When you call `require`, and the module's name is not that of a native module or a file path, Node will automatically look for the file in the `node_modules` folder. This is of course where npm installs modules.

On the next line, we create our Express app by calling the `express` function and assigning it to an `app` variable.

We then create an index route for our application using the `get` method. We specify the path to be `'/'` and then pass in an anonymous function to handle the request. It takes two parameters, the `req` and `res` parameters. Right now, we just write `Hello Express` to the response and return.

We then start our app using the `listen` method and tell it to run on port `3000`. Lastly, we write to the standard output so that we'll know the app has started.

As you can see, the Express magic comes in with setting up routes declaratively. With Express you can easily create routes by specifying an HTTP method, URL path, and a function to handle the request.

Running our application

Let's run our application to see if everything worked. Inside our app folder, type the following on the command-line tool:

```
coffee app.coffee
```

You should see the output as **Listening on port 3000**.

Point your browser to `http://localhost:3000/`. You should see the text **Hello Express**.

To stop the Node process on the command-line tool, just use *Ctrl* + *C*.

Creating a view

Similar to other web frameworks such as Rails, Express has the concepts of views, which let you separate your UI from your application using separate files. Usually, these are written using a templating language such as Jade. Let's create a view for our root action.

To do this, we'll need to:

1. Create a `views` folder and add a Jade view file.
2. Configure our Express application to be aware of a folder where the views will be stored, and which templating library we're using.
3. Change our index route to render our view.

Let's create a new folder in our project root called `views`. Inside this folder, we create a new file named `index.jade`. This is how it should look:

```
doctype 5
html
  head
    title Our Jade view
  body
    p= message
```

As you can see, Jade offers a very clean and terse syntax for normal HTML. You don't have enclosing tags in angle brackets. Similar to CoffeeScript, it also uses indentation to delimit blocks, so that you don't have to enter closing tags. The line `p= message` creates a `<p>` tag whose contents will be evaluated to be the value of the `message` field, which should be passed into our view options.

In our `app.coffee` file, we'll add the following code:

```
express = require 'express'
path = require 'path'
app = express()

app.set 'views', path.join __dirname, 'views'
```

```
app.set 'view engine', 'jade'

app.get '/', (req, res) ->
  res.render 'index', message: "Now we're cooking with gas!"

app.listen(3000)
console.log('Listening on port 3000')
```

Here, we set the `views` folder using the `set` function and assigning the `'views'` key. We use the `path` module that we included at the top of the file to create and join our current folder name to the `views` subfolder. `__dirname` is a global variable that refers to the currently working folder. We also set the view engine to `'jade'`.

Next up, we change our `get '/'` route to render the index template and pass in a hash of options, containing the message. This is the value that then gets rendered in our view.

Once we run our application again and refresh the page, we should now see that our page has been updated with the new text.

node-supervisor

By now, you might be wondering if you'll need to restart our Node application each time we make a change to our code. Ideally in development, we would like our code to be reloaded automatically each time we make a change, similar to how it works in Rails.

Luckily, there is a neat, open source library that we can use that does exactly that: **node-supervisor** (`https://github.com/isaacs/node-supervisor`). We install it like any other npm module, we just make sure to pass the `-g` flag to install it globally, as shown in the following command:

```
npm install supervisor -g
```

In the terminal, you should now be able to run the supervisor by using the following command:

```
supervisor app.coffee
```

Keep this process running in a separate window. To see if this worked, let's edit our message that gets sent to our view; the edited message is highlighted in the following code snippet:

```
app.get '/', (req, res) ->
  res.render 'index', message: "Now we're cooking with supervisor!"
```

If we now refresh our page, we'll see that it has been updated. From here on, we can make sure to keep the supervisor running and we shouldn't need to restart our Node process to make changes.

The to-do list view

Now let's expand our view to look like our real to-do application. Edit the `index.jade` file to look like the following:

```
doctype 5
html
  head
  title Collaborative Todo
  body
    section#todoapp
      header#header
        h1 todos
        input#new-todo(placeholder="What needs to be done?",
autofocus=true)
      section#main
        ul#todo-list
      footer#footer
        button#clear-completed Clear completed
```

Here is some new Jade syntax that we haven't seen before. Tag IDs are denoted by the `#` symbol, so `header#header` becomes `<header id="header">`. Tag attributes are specified within brackets, like so: `tag(name="value")`.

Since we're not using the `message` variable in our template anymore, we'll remove it from our `render` call in the `app.coffee` file, as shown in the following code snippet:

```
app.get '/', (req, res) ->
  res.render 'index'
```

Our page will now be updated, but it won't look too good. We'll use the same stylesheet that we used in the previous project to style our page.

> **Not working as expected?**
>
> Remember to keep an eye on the output of the supervisor process to see if you have any syntax errors in your CoffeeScript or Jade template, especially if you're not seeing the expected output.

Before we use the stylesheet, we need to set up Express to serve static files for us. Modify the `app.coffee` file to look like the following:

```
express = require 'express'
path = require 'path'

app = express()

app.set 'views', path.join __dirname, 'views'
app.set 'view engine', 'jade'
app.use(express.static(path.join __dirname, 'public'))
```

So what's happening in the previous code snippet? We've added support for serving static files in a single line, but how does this work? The answer lies in how Node uses middleware.

Middleware

The Express framework is built on top of a lower-level framework called **Connect** (`http://www.senchalabs.org/connect/`). The basic idea of Connect is to provide middleware for web requests.

Middleware can be chained together to produce a web application stack. Each piece of middleware is only concerned in providing a small set of functionality by modifying the output response or the control flow of the request.

In our example, we tell our application to use the middleware created by the `express.static` function. This function will create a static file server for the provided file path.

Our stylesheet

Create a folder named `public` with a subfolder named `css`. Save the stylesheet as `todo.css` in this folder. We still need to include the stylesheet in our `index` view. Add the following line—highlighted in the code snippet—to the `index.jade` file in the `views` folder:

```
doctype 5
html
  head
  title  Collaborative Todo
  link(rel="stylesheet", href="css/todo.css")
  body
```

Once we have linked to our stylesheet, we should be able to refresh our view. It should now look much nicer.

The client side

To make our to-do application work, we're going to copy the client-side jQuery code that we created in *Chapter 3, CoffeeScript and jQuery*. We're going to put it in a file named `todo.coffee`.

Our next decision is, where shall we put this file? How will we compile and use its output in our application?

We could do the same thing as we did when we built our application in *Chapter 3, CoffeeScript and jQuery*, that is, create a `src` folder containing the client-side offeeScript code, then compile it using the `coffee` command with the `--watch` flag. The outputted JavaScript could then go in our `public` folder where we can include it as normal. But this would mean we would have two separate background tasks running, the supervisor task for running our server and another for compiling our client-side code.

Luckily there is a better way. You might recall that we had a reference to the `connect-assets` module in our `package.json` file. It provides us with an asset pipeline that is very similar to what you get in Rails. It will take care of compilation and dependency management transparently.

We'll need to use the middleware in our `app.coffee` file, as highlighted in the following code snippet:

```
app.set 'views', path.join __dirname, 'views'
app.set 'view engine', 'jade'
app.use(express.static(path.join __dirname, 'public'))
app.use require('connect-assets')()
```

The `connect-assets` module will, by default, use the `assets` folder to manage and serve assets from. Let's create a folder named `assets/js` inside our root folder. We'll create a new file in this folder named `todo.coffee`, containing the following code:

```
Storage::setObj = (key, obj) ->
  localStorage.setItem key, JSON.stringify(obj)

Storage::getObj = (key) ->
  JSON.parse this.getItem(key)

class TodoApp

  constructor: ->
    @cacheElements()
    @bindEvents()
    @displayItems()
```

```
  cacheElements: ->
    @$input = $('#new-todo')
    @$todoList = $('#todo-list')
    @$clearCompleted = $('#clear-completed')

  bindEvents: ->
    @$input.on 'keyup', (e) => @create e
    @$todoList.on 'click', '.destroy', (e) => @destroy e.target
    @$todoList.on 'change', '.toggle', (e) => @toggle e.target
    @$clearCompleted.on 'click', (e) => @clearCompleted()

  create: (e) ->
    val = $.trim @$input.val()
    return unless e.which == 13 and val

    randomId = Math.floor Math.random()*999999

    localStorage.setObj randomId,{
      id: randomId
      title: val
        completed: false
    }
    @$input.val ''
    @displayItems()

  displayItems: ->
    @clearItems()
    @addItem(localStorage.getObj(id)) for id in Object.
keys(localStorage)

  clearItems: ->
    @$todoList.empty()

  addItem: (item) ->
    html = """
      <li #{if item.completed then 'class="completed"' else ''} data-
id="#{item.id}">
        <div class="view">
          <input class="toggle" type="checkbox" #{if item.completed
then 'checked' else ''}>
          <label>#{item.title}</label>
          <button class="destroy"></button>
        </div>
      </li>
```

```
    """
    @$todoList.append html

  destroy: (elem) ->
    id = ($(elem).closest 'li').data('id')
    localStorage.removeItem id
    @displayItems()

  toggle: (elem) ->
    id = $(elem).closest('li').data('id')
    item = localStorage.getObj(id)
    item.completed = !item.completed
    localStorage.setObj(id, item)

  clearCompleted: ->
    (localStorage.removeItem id for id in Object.keys(localStorage) \
      when (localStorage.getObj id).completed)
    @displayItems()

$ ->
  app = new TodoApp()
```

If you were following along in *Chapter 3, CoffeeScript and jQuery*, then this code should be familiar. It's our complete, client-side application that displays to-do items and creates, updates, and destroys items in `localStorage`.

To use this file in our HTML we still need to include a `script` tag. Since we're using jQuery, we'll also need to include the library in our HTML.

Add the following code to the bottom of the `index.jade` file:

```
script(src="//ajax.googleapis.com/ajax/libs/jquery/1.7.2/jquery.min.
js")
!= js('todo')
```

As you can see, we include a link to jQuery using the Google CDN. We then use the `js` helper function, which is provided by `connect-assets`, to create a `script` tag that points to our compiled `todo.js` file (the `connect-assets` module will have compiled our CoffeeScript transparently). The `!=` notation is Jade's syntax for running a JavaScript function along with its result.

If all went well, we should be able to refresh the page and have a working, client-side page for our app. Try adding new items, marking items as complete, deleting items, and clearing completed items.

Adding collaboration

Now we're ready to add collaboration to our to-do list application. We need to create a page where multiple users can connect to the same to-do list and can edit it simultaneously, seeing the results in real time.

We would like to support the idea of named lists, which you can join with others to collaborate on.

Before we dive into the functionality, let's tweak our UI a bit to support all of this.

Creating the collaboration UI

First, we'll add an input field to specify a list name and a button to join the specified list.

Make the following changes (highlighted in the code snippet) to our `index.jade` file, which will add an `input` element and a `button` element to specify our list name and join it:

```
      footer#footer
        | Join list:
        input#join-list-name
        button#join Join
        button#clear-completed Clear completed
    script(src="//ajax.googleapis.com/ajax/libs/jquery/1.7.2/jquery.min.
  js")
    != js('todo')
```

Our page should now look like the page displayed in the following screenshot:

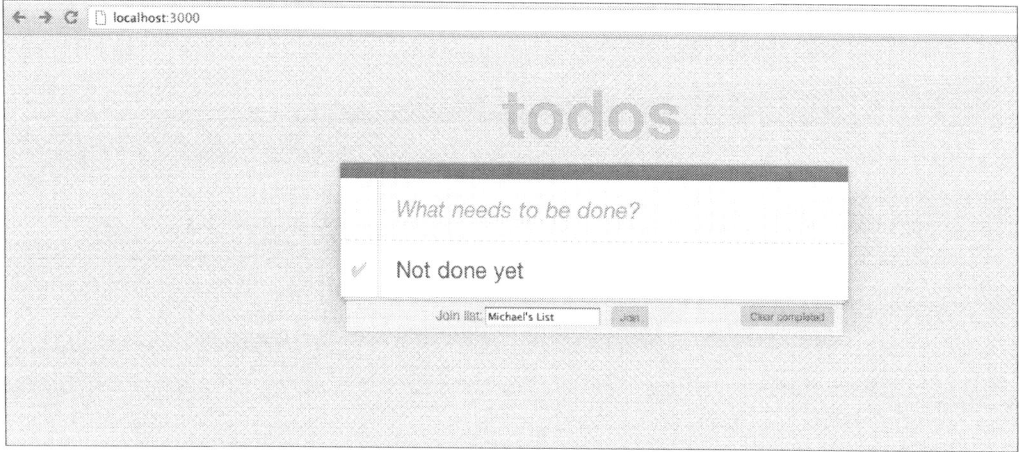

WebSocket on the client

Now let's add an event handler to connect to a room when the user clicks the **Join** button.

In our `todo.coffee` file, we'll add the following code to our `cacheElements` and `bindEvents` functions:

```
cacheElements: ->
    @$input = $('#new-todo')
    @$todoList = $('#todo-list')
    @$clearCompleted = $('#clear-completed')
    @$joinListName = $("#join-list-name")
    @$join = $('#join')

  bindEvents: ->
    @$input.on 'keyup', (e) => @create e
    @$todoList.on 'click', '.destroy', (e) => @destroy e.target
    @$todoList.on  'change', '.toggle', (e) => @toggle e.target
    @$clearCompleted.on 'click', (e) => @clearCompleted()
    @$join.on 'click', (e) => @joinList()
```

We grab the `join-list-name` input and `join` button elements and store them in two instance variables. We then set up the `click` handler on the `@$join` button to call a new function called `joinList`. Let's go ahead and define this function now. Add it to the end of the class after the `bindEvents` function is defined:

```
clearCompleted: ->
    (localStorage.removeItem id for id in Object.keys(localStorage) \
      when (localStorage.getObj id).completed)
    @displayItems()

  joinList: ->
    @socket = io.connect('http://localhost:3000')

    @socket.on 'connect', =>
@socket.emit 'joinList', @$joinListName.val()
```

Here is where we start to use Socket.IO. The Socket.IO library comes in two parts: the client-side library for opening a WebSocket connection, making requests, and receiving responses, as well as the server-side node module for handling the requests.

In the preceding code, the `joinList` function opens a new socket using the `io.connect` function and passing in the URL. It then uses the `on` function to pass a handler function that will run after the WebSocket connection has been made.

The successful connection handler function will in turn use the `socket.emit` function, which allows us to send a custom message to the server using `joinList` as the identifier. We pass the value of the `@joinListName` input as its value.

Before we can start implementing the server-side code, we still need to include a `script` tag to use the `socket.io` client library. Add the following highlighted `script` tag at the bottom of the `index.jade` file:

```
script(src="//ajax.googleapis.com/ajax/libs/jquery/1.7.2/jquery.min.
js")
script(src="/socket.io/socket.io.js")
!= js('todo')
```

You might be wondering where this file comes from. Next, we'll set up the Socket.IO middleware in our `app.coffee` file. This will host the client-side library for us.

WebSocket on the server

We have our client-side code ready to make WebSocket requests; now we can move on to our Node backend. First, we'll need to set up our Socket.IO middleware. There is a small caveat to this, in that we cannot use Socket.IO as a middleware of the Express application directly, since Socket.IO expects a Node.js HTTP server and has no direct support for Express. Instead, we'll create a web server using the built-in Node.js HTTP module, passing our Express application as `requestListener`. We can then use the `listen` function in Socket.IO to connect to the server.

The following is how the code looks in our `app.coffee` file:

```
express = require 'express'
path = require 'path'

app = express()
server = (require 'http').createServer app
io = (require 'socket.io').listen server

app.set 'views', path.join __dirname, 'views'
app.set 'view engine', 'jade'
app.use(express.static(path.join __dirname, 'public'))
app.use (require 'connect-assets')()

app.get '/', (req, res) ->
  res.render 'index'
```

```
io.sockets.on 'connection', (socket) =>
  console.log('connected')
  socket.on 'joinList', (list) => console.log "Joining list #{list}"

server.listen(3000)
console.log('Listening on port 3000')
```

The `io.sockets.on 'connection'` function handles the event when a client connects. Here, we log to the console that we're connected to and then set up the `joinList` message handler. Right now, we'll just log the value that we receive from the client to the console.

We should now be able to test connecting to a list. Refresh our to-do list home page and enter a list name to join. After you clicked the **Join** button, head over to our background supervisor task. You should see something similar to the following message:

connected

Joining list Michael's List

It worked! We've successfully created a bi-directional WebSocket connection. We still haven't really joined a list so far, so let's go ahead and do that now.

Joining a list

To join a list, we'll use a feature of Socket.IO called **rooms**. It allows the Socket.IO server to segment its clients and emit messages to subsets of all the connected clients. On the server, we'll keep track of the to-do lists of each room and then tell the client to sync its local list when connected.

We'll update the `app.coffee` file with the highlighted code shown in the following code snippet:

```
@todos = {}
io.sockets.on 'connection', (socket) =>
  console.log('connected')
  socket.on 'joinList', (list) =>
    console.log "Joining list #{list}"
    socket.list = list
    socket.join(list)
    @todos[list] ?= []
    socket.emit 'syncItems', @todos[list]
```

We initialize the `@todos` instance variable to be an empty hash. It will hold the to-do lists for each room, using the list name as a key. In the `joinList` handler function, we set the `list` property of the `socket` variable to equal the list name that the client passed in.

We then use the `socket.join` function that will join our list to a room with that name. If the room doesn't exist yet, it will be created. We then assign an empty array value to the item in `@todos` with the key equal to `list`. The `?=` operator will only assign the value on the right-hand side to the object on the left-hand side if it's `null`.

Lastly, we send a message to the client using the `socket.emit` function. The `syncItems` identifier will tell it to sync its local data with the to-do list items that we're passing it.

To handle the `syncItems` message, we'll need to update the `todo.coffee` file with the following highlighted code:

```
joinList: ->
  @socket = io.connect('http://localhost:3000')
  @socket.on 'connect', =>
 @socket.emit 'joinList', @$joinListName.val()

  @socket.on 'syncItems', (items) =>
    @syncItems(items)


syncItems: (items) ->
  console.log 'syncing items'
  localStorage.clear()
  localStorage.setObj item.id, item for item in items
  @displayItems()
```

After joining a list, we set up our client connection to handle the `syncItems` message. We expect to receive all the to-do items for the list that we have just joined. The `syncItems` function will clear all the current items in `localStorage`, add all the new items, and then display them.

The UI

Lastly, let's update our UI so that the user will know when they've joined a list and let them leave it. We'll modify our `#footer div` tag as follows in our `index.jade` file:

```
doctype 5
html
  head
```

```
    title  Collaborative Todo
    link(rel="stylesheet", href="css/todo.css")
    body
      section#todoapp
        header#header
          h1 todos
          input#new-todo(placeholder="What needs to be done?",
autofocus=true)
        section#main
          ul#todo-list
        footer#footer
          section#connect
            | Join list:
            input#join-list-name
            button#join Join
            button#clear-completed Clear completed
          section#disconnect.hidden
            | Joined list:  
            span#connected-list List name
            button#leave Leave
      script(src="//ajax.googleapis.com/ajax/libs/jquery/1.7.2/jquery.
min.js")
      script(src="/socket.io/socket.io.js")
      != js('todo')
```

In the previous markup, we've added two new sections to our `footer div` tag. Each section will either be hidden or visible depending on which state we are in, `connected` or `disconnected` from a list. The `connect` section is the same as before. The `disconnect` section will display which list you are currently connected to and has a **Leave** button.

Now we'll add code to our `todo.coffee` file to update the UI when a list is joined.

First, we'll cache the new elements in our `cacheElements` function, as highlighted in the following code snippet:

```
cacheElements: ->
    @$input = $('#new-todo')
    @$todoList = $('#todo-list')
    @$clearCompleted = $('#clear-completed')
    @$joinListName = $("#join-list-name")
    @$join = $('#join')
    @$connect = $('#connect')
    @$disconnect = $('#disconnect')
    @$connectedList = $('#connected-list')
    @$leave = $('#leave')
```

Next, we'll change the UI to display that we're in a `connected` state when `syncItems` have been called (which gets fired by the server after successfully joining a list). We use the `@currentList` function, which we'll set in the `joinList` function; add the code highlighted in the following code snippet:

```
joinList: ->
  @socket = io.connect('http://localhost:3000')
  @socket.on 'connect', =>
    @currentList = @$joinListName.val()
    @socket.emit 'joinList', @currentList

  @socket.on 'syncItems', (items) => @syncItems(items)

syncItems: (items) ->
  console.log 'syncing items'
  localStorage.clear()
  localStorage.setObj item.id, item for item in items
  @displayItems()
  @displayConnected(@currentList)

displayConnected: (listName) ->
  @$disconnect.removeClass 'hidden'
  @$connectedList.text listName
  @$connect.addClass 'hidden'
```

The `displayConnected` function will just hide the `connect` section and show the `disconnect` section.

Leaving a list

Leaving a list should be quite easy. We disconnect the current socket connection and then update the UI.

To handle the `disconnect` action when a button is clicked, we add a handler in our `bindEvents` function, as shown in the following code snippet:

```
bindEvents: ->
    @$input.on 'keyup', (e) => @create e
    @$todoList.on 'click', '.destroy', (e) => @destroy e.target
    @$todoList.on  'change', '.toggle', (e) => @toggle e.target
    @$clearCompleted.on 'click', (e) => @clearCompleted()
    @$join.on 'click', (e) => @joinList()
    @$leave.on 'click', (e) => @leaveList()
```

As you can see, the handler we've added will just call a `leaveList` function. We still need to implement it. Add the following two functions to the end of the class after the last function defined in our `TodoApp` class:

```
leaveList: ->
  @socket.disconnect() if @socket
  @displayDisconnected()

 displayDisconnected: () ->
  @$disconnect.addClass 'hidden'
  @$connect.removeClass 'hidden'
```

Testing it all

Now let's test our list joining and leaving code. To see it all in action, follow these steps:

1. Open `http://localhost:3000/` in your browser.
2. In the browser window, type a list name and hit **Join List**. The UI should update as expected.
3. Once you've joined a list, add a few to-do items.
4. Now open the site again, this time using a second browser. Since `localStorage` is unique to a browser, we do this to have a clean list of to-do items.
5. Once again, type the same list name as you did in the other browser and hit **Join List**.
6. As the list is synced, you should now see the list items you've added in before showing up.

7. Lastly, disconnect from a list using the **Leave** button.

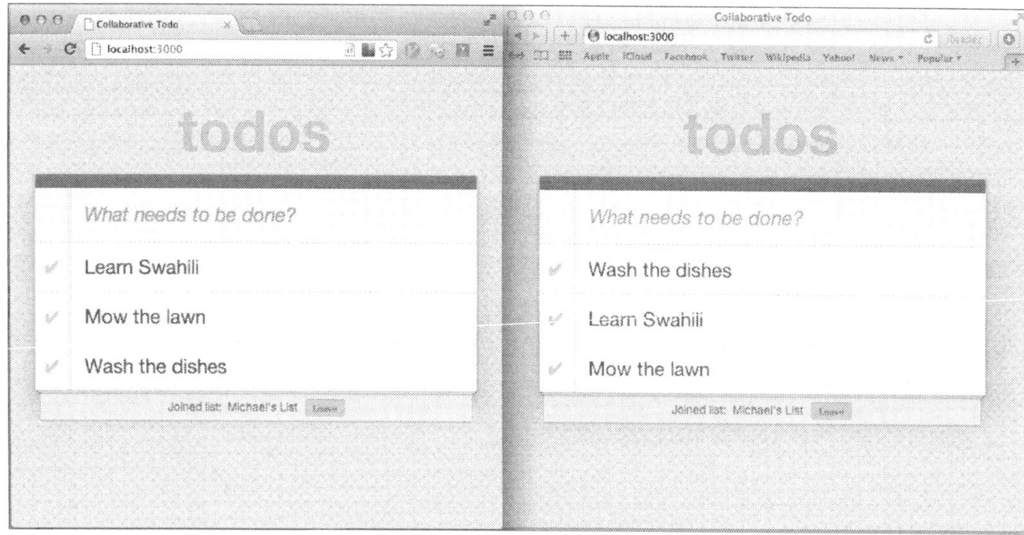

Two lists synced from different browsers

This is great! We can now see the power of WebSockets in action. Our client is notified when it should sync items without having to poll the server.

However, once we're connected to the list, we still cannot add new items to have them show up in all the other clients in the room. Let's implement that.

Adding to-do items to a shared list

First, we'll handle adding new items on the server. The best place to handle this would be in the existing `create` function for creating to-do items. Instead of just adding them to `localStorage`, we'll also emit a message to the server telling it that a new to-do item has been created, and pass it as a parameter. Modify the `create` function to look like the following code:

```
create: (e) ->
    val = $.trim @$input.val()
    return unless e.which == 13 and val

    randomId = Math.floor Math.random()*999999

    newItem =
       id: randomId
       title: val
```

```
      completed: false

    localStorage.setObj randomId, newItem
    @socket.emit 'newItem', newItem if @socket
    @$input.val ''
    @displayItems()
```

We need to handle the `newItem` message on the server. We'll set up the code to do so when a client joins a list, in `app.coffee`.

Let's modify the `joinList` event handler that we added before; add the highlighted code in the following code snippet:

```
io.sockets.on 'connection', (socket) =>
  console.log("connected")
  socket.on 'joinList', (list) =>
    console.log "Joining list #{list}"
    socket.list = list
    socket.join(list)
    @todos[list] ?= []

    socket.emit 'syncItems', @todos[list]

    socket.on 'newItem', (todo) =>
      console.log "new todo #{todo.title}"
      @todos[list].push todo
      io.sockets.in(socket.list).emit('itemAdded', todo)
```

In this code snippet, we set up yet another `socket` event when a user joins a list. In this case, it's for the `newItem` event. We add the new to-do item to our `@todos` array using the `push` function. Then we emit a new `itemAdded` message to all the clients in the current list.

What will happen with this `itemAdded` message? You guessed it; it will get handled in the client again. This kind of back and forth messaging is very common in WebSocket applications and does take some getting used to. Don't fret though; it gets easier once you get the hang of it.

Meanwhile let's handle the `itemAdded` event on the client. We also set up this code in our `joinList` method by adding the highlighted code in the following code snippet:

```
joinList: ->
    @socket = io.connect('http://localhost:3000')
    @socket.on 'connect', =>
      @currentList = @$joinListName.val()
      @socket.emit 'joinList', @currentList
```

```
        @socket.on 'syncItems', (items) => @syncItems(items)

        @socket.on 'itemAdded', (item) =>
          localStorage.setObj item.id, item
          @displayItems()
```

We handle the `itemAdded` event by calling `localStorage.setObject` with the item ID and value. This will either create a new to-do item if it's not present in `localStorage`, or it will update the existing value.

And that's it! We should now be able to add items to all the clients in the list. To test it, we'll follow similar steps to what we did earlier:

1. Open `http://localhost:3000/` in your browser.
2. In the browser window, type a list name and hit **Join List**. The UI should update as expected.
3. Now open the site again, this time using a second browser.
4. Once again, type the same list name as you did in the other browser and hit **Join List**.
5. Add new to-do items in either browser. You'll see the to-do items appear in the other browser immediately.

Wow! Isn't this impressive?

Removing to-do items from a shared list

To remove to-do items from a shared list, we'll follow a similar pattern to adding items. In the `destroy` function in `todo.coffee`, we'll emit a `removeItem` message to our socket to let the server know that a item should be removed, as shown in the following code snippet:

```
destroy: (elem) ->
    id = ($(elem).closest 'li').data('id')
    localStorage.removeItem id
    @socket.emit 'removeItem', id if @socket
    @displayItems()
```

Once again, we set up the server-side code to handle this message by removing the item from the shared list in memory, and then notify all clients connected to the list that the item has been removed:

```
io.sockets.on 'connection', (socket) =>
  console.log("connected")
  socket.on 'joinList', (list) =>
```

```
    console.log "Joining list #{list}"
    socket.list = list
    socket.join(list)
    @todos[list] ?= []

    socket.emit 'syncItems', @todos[list]

    socket.on 'newItem', (todo) =>
      console.log "new todo #{todo.title}"
      @todos[list].push todo
      io.sockets.in(socket.list).emit('itemAdded', todo)

    socket.on 'removeItem', (id) =>
      @todos[list] = @todos[list].filter (item) -> item.id isnt id
      io.sockets.in(socket.list).emit('itemRemoved', id)
```

The `removeItem` socket event handler gets the ID of the to-do item to remove the task passed into it. It removes the to-do item from the list by assigning the current value of the shared list to a new value that we create using JavaScript's array `filter` function. This will select all the items that don't have the passed ID. It then calls `emit` on all the client socket connections in the shared list with the `itemRemoved` message.

Lastly, we'll need to handle the `itemRemoved` message in our client. Similar to when we added items, we'll set this up in the `joinList` function in `todo.coffee`, as shown in the following code snippet:

```
joinList: ->
    @socket = io.connect('http://localhost:3000')
    @socket.on 'connect', =>
      @currentList = @$joinListName.val()
      @socket.emit 'joinList', @currentList

    @socket.on 'syncItems', (items) => @syncItems(items)

    @socket.on 'itemAdded', (item) =>
      localStorage.setObj item.id, item
      @displayItems()

    @socket.on 'itemRemoved', (id) =>
      localStorage.removeItem id
      @displayItems()
```

We remove the item from `localStorage` and update the UI.

To test removing items, follow these steps:

1. Open `http://localhost:3000/` in your browser.
2. In the browser window, type a list name and hit **Join List**. The UI should update as expected.
3. Once you've connected to the shared list, add a few to-do items.
4. Now open the site again, this time using a second browser.
5. Once again, type the same list name as you did in the other browser and hit **Join List**. Your to-do list will be synced with the shared list and will contain the items that you have added in the other browser.
6. Click the remove icon to delete to-do items in either browser. You'll see the deleted to-do items disappear in the other browser immediately.

Now, it's your turn

As a final exercise to you, I will ask you to make the **Clear completed** button work. As a hint, you should be able to use the existing `destroyItem` method functionality.

Summary

In this chapter, we completed our tour of the CoffeeScript ecosystem by exploring Node.js as a fast, event-driven platform that lets you use JavaScript or CoffeeScript to write server applications. I hope that you have been given a glimpse of the joy of being able to write web applications using CoffeeScript on the server as well as in the browser at the same time.

We also spent some time with some of the wonderful open source libraries and frameworks that have been written for Node.js, like expressjs, connect, and Socket.IO and have seen how we can successfully use npm to manage dependencies and modules in our applications.

Our sample application was exactly the kind of thing that you would use Node.js for, and we saw how its event-driven model lends itself to writing applications where there are lots of constant interactions between the client and server.

Now that we've come to an end to our journey, I hope to have instilled in you the eagerness and skills to go out and use CoffeeScript to change the world. We've spent some time exploring not just the language but also the wonderful tools, libraries, and frameworks that enable us to develop powerful applications more rapidly using less code.

The future of CoffeeScript and the JavaScript ecosystem is bright, and hopefully you'll be a part of it!

Index

Symbols

$(document).ready event handler 63
$(document).ready() function 59
@$input 68
$@todoList 69
.coffee files
  running 52
@displayItems 71
@displayItems() 67
@joinListName 110
@name instance variable 34
@odometer 18
@ symbol 33
=> symbol 33

A

action function 34
addItem method 69
Apple installer
  using 44, 45
ApplicationController class 80
apt-get package manager 48
arguments 12
array slicing 29
array splicing 29

B

Basecamp 73
bindEvents method 63, 67
birthday class 34
block comments 36
block strings 36
braces 9

C

cacheElements method 68
chained comparisons 36
class syntax 18
client side, Node.js application 105
closest function 71
coffee command
  about 51
  options 51
  uses 51
coffee command, options
  .coffee files, running 52
  compiling to JavaScript 53
  REPL 52
  watch 53
CoffeeScript
  about 7
  array, slicing 29
  array, splicing 29
  chained comparisons 36
  compiling, to JavaScript 53
  conditional clauses 28
  features 7
  function arguments 12, 13
  function syntax 11
  installing, on Linux 48
  installing, on Mac 44
  installing, on Windows 43
  jQuery, working with 58
  logical aliases 28

Node.js, working with 96
object syntax 16
Rails, working with 75
scopes, handling 14
switch statements 35
using 51
CoffeeScript compiler
working 40
CoffeeScript installation, on Linux
about 48
Debian 48
other distributions 48
Ubuntu and MintOS 48
with npm 49
CoffeeScript installation, on Mac
about 44
Apple installer, used 44, 45
Homebrew, used 46
with npm 47
CoffeeScript installation, on Windows 41
CoffeeScript solutions
equality operator 21
existential operator 22, 23
reserved words and object syntax, using 19
string concatenation 21
CoffeeScript stack 39
CoffeeScript syntax
about 8, 9
braces 9
parenthesis 10
semicolons 9
whitespace 9
CoffeeScript view, Rails application
adding 91
collaboration, Node.js application
adding 108
collaboration UI, Node.js application
creating 108
conditional clauses 28
Connect
about 104
URL 104
Content Delivery Network (CDN) 58
controller, Rails application 80
createItem method 67
create method 64
CSS, Rails application 82

D

data-id attribute 70
db*migrate 85
Debian 48
destructuring
about 30
using 31, 32
displayConnected function 114
displayItems method 66
Don't repeat yourself (DRY) 74

E

each iterator 87
equality operator 21
ERB templates 87
EventMachine 95
existential operator 22
Express
about 97
URL 97
express.static function 104
extends operator 18

F

filter function 119
form_for method 90
for statement 25
function arguments 12, 13
function syntax 11

G

gems 75
getLocation function 31
greet function 14

H

Homebrew
using 46
http-server
URL 61

I

installation
CoffeeScript, on Linux 48
CoffeeScript, on Mac 44
CoffeeScript, on Windows 41
Rails 76
items, jQuery application
completing 71
removing 70
items, Rails application
adding 89, 90
displaying 87

J

Jade 98
JavaScript
Rails, working with 74, 75
javascript_include_tag method 82
joinList 109
jQuery
$ function 56
about 55
Ajax methods 58
element, changing 56
element, finding 56
using 58
utility functions 57
working, with CoffeeScript 58
jQuery application
app.coffee file, creating 59, 60
CoffeeScript, compiling 58, 59
initial HTML 62
initializing 63
items, completing 71
items, removing 70
local web server, running 61
testing 60
to-do item, adding 64
to-do item, displaying 66-69
TodoMVC 62

K

keyup event 64

L

Law of Demeter 23
Linux
CoffeeScript, installing 48
Linux or Unix
prerequisites, for building Node.js 49
list comprehensions
about 24-27
for statement 25
using 28
while loop 24
list, Node.js application
joining 111, 112
leaving 114
testing 115, 116
UI 112, 113
localStorage
about 64
using 64-66
logical aliases 28

M

Mac
CoffeeScript, installing 44
metaprogramming 74
Middleware 104
migration, Rails application 84, 85
model, Rails application 83
MRI 76
multiplesOf function 27
MVC 62

N

Node 39
Node.js
about 39, 40, 95
building 49
building, on Linux or Unix 49
building, on Windows 50
downloading 41, 42
features 95
installing 40-43
installing, on Windows 41
working, with CoffeeScript 96

Node.js application
building 98
client side 105, 107
collaboration, adding 108
collaboration UI, creating 108
creating 100
Hello World 96, 97
list, joining 111
modules, installing 99
node-supervisor 102
package.json 99
running 100
to-do items, adding to shared list 116, 117
to-do items, removing from shared list 118-120
to-do list view 103
view, creating 101, 102
WebSocket, on client 109
WebSocket, on server 110, 111
writing 96
Node.js wiki
URL 41
node-supervisor
about 102
URL 102
npm
about 40
installing 40, 43

O

object inheritance 17, 18
object syntax
about 16, 17
prototypes, extending 18
opinionated framework 73

P

package.json 99
parenthesis 10
partial, Rails application
creating 88, 89
pattern matching 30
Person object 34
prepare function 34
prerequisites, for building Node.js on Linux or Unix
libssl-dev 49
Python 49

R

Rails
about 73
convention over configuration 73, 74
Don't repeat yourself (DRY) 74
features 73
installing 76
installing, RailsInstaller used 76
installing, RVM used 76
working, with CoffeeScript 75, 76
working, with JavaScript 74, 75
Rails application
CoffeeScript view, adding 91
controller 80
CSS 82
developing 77, 78
items, adding 89, 90
items, displaying 87, 88
migration 84
model 83
MVC 78
partial, creating 88, 89
Rails console 85, 86
routes.rb 80
running 78
tasks, removing 93
to-do item, adding 90
to-do items, completing 92
todo_items resource 79
view 81, 82
Rails console 85
Rails installation
about 76
RailsInstaller, used 76
RVM, used 76
RailsInstaller
about 76
URL 76
Read Eval Print Loop (REPL) 52
removeItem socket event handler 119

requestListener 110
return keyword 12
rooms 111
routes.rb file, Rails application 80
RVM
  about 76
  URL 76

S

salutation variable 14
scopes, handling 14
semicolons 9
socket.emit function 110
splats 13
string concatenation 21
strings 36
stylesheet_link_tag method 82
switch statements 35

T

tasks, Rails application
  removing 93
this keyword 33
TodoApp class 63
to-do item, jQuery application
  adding 64
  displaying 66-69
TodoItem model 83
to-do item, Rails application
  adding 90
  completing 92, 93
TodoItemsController 79
to-do items, Node.js application
  adding, to shared list 116, 117
  removing, from shared list 118, 119
todo_items resource, Rails application 79
to-do list view, Node.js application
  expanding 103
  Middleware 104
  stylesheet 104
TodoMVC 62
Tornado 95
t.timestamps method 84
Twisted 95

U

Ubuntu and MintOS 48
until keyword 25

V

val() function 64
var keyword 14, 15
view, Node.js application
  creating 101, 102
view partial 88
views, Rails application 81

W

WebSocket
  about 97
  on client 109
  on server 110
while loop 24
whitespace 9, 10
window object 15
Windows
  CoffeeScript, installing 41
  Node.js, building 50

Thank you for buying
CoffeeScript Programming with jQuery, Rails, and Node.js

About Packt Publishing

Packt, pronounced 'packed', published its first book "*Mastering phpMyAdmin for Effective MySQL Management*" in April 2004 and subsequently continued to specialize in publishing highly focused books on specific technologies and solutions.

Our books and publications share the experiences of your fellow IT professionals in adapting and customizing today's systems, applications, and frameworks. Our solution based books give you the knowledge and power to customize the software and technologies you're using to get the job done. Packt books are more specific and less general than the IT books you have seen in the past. Our unique business model allows us to bring you more focused information, giving you more of what you need to know, and less of what you don't.

Packt is a modern, yet unique publishing company, which focuses on producing quality, cutting-edge books for communities of developers, administrators, and newbies alike. For more information, please visit our website: `www.packtpub.com`.

About Packt Open Source

In 2010, Packt launched two new brands, Packt Open Source and Packt Enterprise, in order to continue its focus on specialization. This book is part of the Packt Open Source brand, home to books published on software built around Open Source licences, and offering information to anybody from advanced developers to budding web designers. The Open Source brand also runs Packt's Open Source Royalty Scheme, by which Packt gives a royalty to each Open Source project about whose software a book is sold.

Writing for Packt

We welcome all inquiries from people who are interested in authoring. Book proposals should be sent to author@packtpub.com. If your book idea is still at an early stage and you would like to discuss it first before writing a formal book proposal, contact us; one of our commissioning editors will get in touch with you.

We're not just looking for published authors; if you have strong technical skills but no writing experience, our experienced editors can help you develop a writing career, or simply get some additional reward for your expertise.

Made in the USA
Lexington, KY
26 September 2013